When God Was Little

Luke Knight

2014 by Luke Knight

ISBN # 978-1-312-61435-2
whengodwaslittle.com

Editor	Aimee Ouellette
Design	Jeff Law
Publishing	Devan Sylvester
Cover	Danaea Li Photography
Website	Jeff Law

DEDICATION

For my cousin Emma, who was brave enough to ask
and humble enough to listen; bravery and humility
is what Christmas is all about.

For my parents, who always made Christmas special.

ACKNOWLEDGMENTS

To say this little book was a collaboration would be a massive understatement.

Thanks to Jeff and Dani Law and Devan Sylvester whose support has been overwhelming. This project wouldn't exist without their expertise and diligence. Thanks to Aimee Ouellette, my friend and editor. Her humility and generosity has wonderfully embodied the heart of this content. Special thanks to Kieran and Miles for graciously sharing their partner/mommy with our endeavour.

Thanks to Justin and Kaela Napier for their notes and encouragement. Thanks to Esanju Bonga, Elyse and Christian Brouwer, Danaea Davies, Trisha Donkers and Shannon Smith for their willingness to serve this project as unassumingly they did. Thanks to Rikk and Katie Watts for allowing me to roam freely with some of their thoughts. Their content and character is peppered throughout this work.

Thanks to Doug and Linda Smith whose many years of investment in my life are reflected in these pages. If I can learn to love people half as well as they do one day, I'll be a happy camper. Thanks to the team at LWC who've let me expand on our recent holiday collaboration. They're the best. Thanks to my church, whom I love with all my heart, which has consequently grown three sizes since we were first acquainted.

Special thanks to my parents, Brian and Trisha Donkers and Reuben and Lisa Kramer for the never-ending (almost annoying) amount of encouragement.

CONTENTS

Preface

11

Part One

What's with this Kid?

15

Part Two

Birth Stories

25

Part Three

First Impressions

39

Part Four

Intergalactic Infant

49

Part Five

Never Break Character

61

Part Six

Grasping Greatness

77

Part Seven

Making Room

91

PREFACE

Last winter I walked down a street in my town and spotted something in a storefront window that gave me pause. I peered inside to take a closer look. There before me was a delightful, ten-inch figurine of Santa Claus. In his arms he cradled a soundly sleeping baby Jesus. I would have snatched it up, had it not been a little pricey. Two thousand years of culture, fact and fiction merged before me in pure ceramic brilliance. I may have missed a truly golden retail opportunity.

Since his birth, somewhere near the beginning of the first century, we've thought about and pictured Jesus many different ways. How do you picture him?

This question undoubtedly stirs up plenty of images. Found amongst them, perhaps, is a be-haloed infant nestled in a bunch of hay. That Jesus was a baby is both a confounding mystery and an inspiring notion (depending on who you think he was, of course).

There's always been great debate concerning Jesus' true identity. In the midst of this debate, however, millions around the world continue to celebrate seasons like Christmas and Easter, and most agree that Jesus has at least a little to do with these two particular holidays.

A primary story we tell and celebrate at Christmas surrounds the *birth* of Jesus. We learn about his infancy and adult life in the Bible, a collection of writings from dozens of authors, penned over hundreds of years. Four books in the Bible, called the gospels, give us Jesus' life story.

The gospel accounts of Jesus' life tell us two things, amongst others, that the rest of the Bible's New Testament corroborates: Jesus was born, and Jesus was human; just like you and me. We find ourselves in good and abounding company if this throws us for somewhat of a loop. If the Bible clearly states that Jesus was human, what do we do with all the God *stuff* surrounding his story?

When some friends heard I was writing a book, they asked what it was about. I told them: "It's a book about baby Jesus." A number of them followed up their first question with a second: "Is it for kids?" I said that it wasn't, and then rather puzzled looks slowly spread over their faces. Once a barista at a local coffee shop inquired about what I was writing. I tried describing the project in a less direct manner, just to keep things simple. "It's about Christmas." I said. "Oh, like a children's book?" She replied.

There's no getting around it. We tend to associate Christmas with children, and rightly so. Thinking like a child is, in part, helpful in understanding Christmas according to its biblical roots. Kids are filled with wonder and aren't afraid to ask questions. Grown-ups would do well to learn from kids in this regard.

I work in the quaint village of Fort Langley, British Columbia. It's full of antique stores, artisan workshops, restaurants and coffee shops. Fort Langley is quaint, but rarely quiet. The village is a favourable shooting location for film and television productions, particularly Christmas movies. Almost any time of the year you can wander into a Christmas film set, even in the middle of August, fake snow and all. Fort Langley is a year-round Christmas town.

The discussion surrounding exactly when Jesus was born in the calendar year is robust. Some say it could have been in December, others hold it was in the spring. It may not really matter. Just like I can wander onto a Christmas film set in Fort Langley at any time of the year, we can investigate and experience the message and meaning of Christmas any time we like, too.

The birth and infancy of Jesus are also not events we can discuss in a vacuum. In order to fully appreciate Jesus we must consider his whole story. Jesus' origins are important, and we'll examine those throughout the book, but we'll also draw from the rest of his life and the broader biblical narrative.

Some readers are totally comfortable with the notion that Jesus was not *just* a man but also "God in the flesh." If you live in that world, welcome. I hope you'll be inspired as you think about Jesus, God, babies and hay.

Others of us aren't so sure about a *Godly* Jesus, and so a divine infant can sound a little far-fetched. We may not be completely comfortable with a Christian world view. We may even question whether we should be propping up dead trees, eating copious amounts of stuffing and giving each other gifts in Jesus' honour to mark the big day in the first place. If you live in that world, thanks for choosing this book over television. You may not be aware of this, but you're actually amongst a small percentage of people intentionally and honestly asking big and brave questions about Jesus. I admire and applaud your curiosity. Maybe you're not sure what to think about the baby in the manger, and that's okay—this little book won't ask you to make up your mind about him by Christmas morning—I'm just happy you're giving Jesus some thought.

Regardless of what each of us thinks about Jesus' true nature, let's reflect on his infancy and some of his adult life *together*. We'll ask questions like:

How did Jesus' life start?

What made Jesus so special?

How does Jesus' life potentially inform our view of the divine?

The most famous and influential figure to emerge from the ancient world, if not all of history, tends to inspire wonder and induce contemplation around the holiday season. His extraordinary life, we are told, began in a barn.

Happy Holidays and Merry Christmas,

Luke Knight

Part One
What's With This Kid?

Who are you? Who, who, who, who?
-The Who, "Who Are You?"

Who was Jesus, really?

One of my favourite Christmas carols is by an English writer named William Chatterton Dix. The story goes that at age twenty-nine he wrote "What Child is This?" after suffering through serious illness and wrestling with deep depression.[1] The lyrics we sing today echo a question people have been asking about Jesus for centuries: *what's with this kid*?

I've noticed two spectacles that inspire wonder in people, and induce an almost hypnotic effect: campfires and babies. People are drawn to combustion and cradles; they share some similar traits. Both instill wonder and curiosity, both cause us to reflect on life and meaning, and both have the power to make us feel extremely uneasy. Fires and babies are unpredictable, keeping us on our toes.

The baby Jesus has stirred similar sentiments in many over the years. He can inspire wonder, causing us to reflect on the deep matters of life. He can also tend to make us feel a little uncomfortable.

Few dispute Jesus existed. An immense amount of biblical and extra-biblical evidence testifies that he lived. We have reliable, historical documentation on Jesus that far outweighs our evidence for many other famous, ancient figures. Jesus' historicity has been thoroughly tried and tested.[2]

Credible historians and scholars agree: Jesus lived, and obviously

15

made a tremendous impact on the world. Two millennia later we're still talking about him.

Most Buddhist, Hindu, Islamic, Jewish and Sikh thinkers don't discredit Jesus' existence either. In fact, he's revered in several of the world's major religions. Christians aren't the only people intrigued by Jesus. The Dalai Lama has great respect for Jesus, and even wrote a book about his teachings.[3]

Opinions concerning Jesus' identity range widely. Muslims believe Jesus to be a great prophet, though they don't agree we should worship him. Jewish scholars have numerous perspectives on Jesus; maybe he was just a prophet, or a superb teacher, or a heretic.

Weren't you born in a barn?

Christians think differently about Jesus. They believe Jesus was more than human, but divine *and* human. They also believe he literally died on a cross, later resurrecting from the dead. Many today find that a bit of stretch. Here's why.

First of all, the idea that there even is a God is very much up for debate. In some circles God's coffin is already securely six feet under, so to speak. And, if there is a God, how can we be sure that "God" can be defined or understood? Some argue over whether or not we're able to prove that walls exist. Where do we begin with God?

Second, to concede that a God-man walked the earth when Caesar Augustus did can feel antiquated. That Mary gave birth to Jesus despite being a virgin is also a leap for us. Every now and then we hear of women who go into labour and had no idea they were pregnant. These kinds of abnormal occurrences are hard to believe; yet they happen. A *virgin* having a baby is a whole other story—let alone a virgin giving birth to a divine baby.

These events and claims are miraculous and challenging to accept. A small, radical first-century gang may have propagated the divine-Jesus rumour at first, but that was some time ago. Jesus lived over two thousand years ago, and people looked at the world differently than we do now.

A god-man wasn't a stretch for ancient people, at least not theoretically. Despite this fact, however, Jesus' way of life and claims about himself were deeply challenging for his contemporaries.

Some philosophers rejected the pantheon of gods worshipped by the masses, even though it may have landed them in hot water, but most people had no problem accepting supernatural ideologies. People were spiritual back then. Lots of us still are. If you asked someone in my neighbourhood if they were religious, there's a good chance they'd say no. Quite a few, however, would agree that they're spiritual.[4]

That supernatural events occurred, and that the gods engaged somewhat with life on earth, was pervasive thinking in the days of Moses, Cleopatra and Cyrus the Great. There was more to the world, people thought, than met the eye. Natural and supernatural commingled in ancient thought.

Despite this merging, however, many ancient people thought of the gods as detached and generally unconcerned with everyday human life. Commingling occurred, but it usually revolved around divine self-interest. Belief that the gods *intermingled* with people (to put it tastefully) was also common. Half-gods or part-gods are all over the place in early lore; Hercules and Achilles are good examples from the Greeks. Sometimes rulers or kings were considered gods, like the Egyptian pharaohs. They built giant statues all over the place to keep people in line, and remind them who was boss.

The great Julius Caesar was deified (post-mortem). This worked out rather nicely for his would-be successor, Octavian (known better as Caesar Augustus, Rome's emperor on the day Jesus was born). When Octavian had his eye on the empire, he used his relationship with Julius Caesar to his advantage.

> His [Octavian's] standing was considerably enhanced, for he could style himself *divi filius*, the son of a god. His supporters lost no opportunity to publicize his adoptive father's elevation to the stars.[5]

So what makes Jesus, a self-proclaimed God-man, unique? What separates Jesus from the mighty pharaohs, or Heracles, or the Caesars, or all the great prophets and thinkers of old? What makes him stand out from the rest?[6] Why was Jesus' life and message challenging for those who knew him?

Jesus is different because he *wasn't* great. Jesus never led an army and never ruled a nation. Also, his friends didn't claim he was just a great teacher or prophet. Nor did they say he was half-god, half-human, or mostly human with a dash of god. Jesus' friends believed he was fully God (the only and one-true God, with a capital G) and fully human.

At the time, both the Jewish world Jesus emerged from, and the Greek-speaking one in which his story spread, uttered a collective response to this claim: *Huh? Wasn't this guy born in a barn? Didn't he die on a cross?*

Many have shown that a human claiming to be the one-true God of the universe was quite odd, even for the ancient world, and especially for a human like Jesus. Ancient rulers had PR departments who would spin divine-nature stories with flare, and thus these leaders demanded submission. They also had swords, chariots and armies, which certainly aided in establishing control over their subjects. After all, aren't gods meant to be strong?

No one had ever heard of a god or a king who lived with humility and chose to ask if you'd like to submit to him or not.[7] Jesus' life and message was as challenging to ancient people as it is to us today.

The stuff of legend.

Jesus hailed from a rural fishing village and probably worked most of his life as a tradesperson. He then garnered a minor following in a dusty corner of the Roman Empire plagued with uprisings and rebellions. Most of his followers bailed when he was arrested and sentenced to the cruellest form of capital punishment Rome dealt out. Jesus didn't look good on paper.

A Jewish man named Paul was one of Christianity's earliest and most important thinkers. The record of his travels, found in the biblical book of Acts, says he experienced a lot of opposition when he told people who he thought Jesus was.

Once, at a spot in modern-day Turkey, an angry mob dragged Paul outside the city, stoned him, and left him for dead, all because he wouldn't shut up about Jesus' divinity. After regaining consciousness, he got up and went back inside to give it another go. Acts tells us people would follow Paul from place to place just to give him a hard time.[8] Talk about dedicated hecklers.

Ancient people may have been more open to the supernatural than we in the West are today, but the first Christians' claims (that Jesus was divine and literally resurrected from the dead) were no less disturbing.[9] It sounded wacky.

Neither the mythic gods of Greece nor the historical rulers of Egypt hung around with regular folks, shared finger food at parties or climbed into boats for a snooze. They certainly didn't strip down to their skivvies to wash a bunch of smelly fishermen's feet either. This didn't sound like something the great Achilles might list as a hobby. The gospel accounts say Jesus did all of these things.

Most ancient gods were fantastic. Stories about them are slotted into a literary category we call *mythology*. The Greeks had one of the more diverse pantheons in history. In reality their gods were just a reflection of the Greeks themselves. A scholar friend of mine says the gods generally looked like "Greeks on steroids." This is why they're as selfish and self-absorbed as you and me. They're a reflection of us, just in high definition.

When Paul travelled to the city of Athens with his teachings about Jesus, he got the chance to chat with the most intelligent and powerful people in the city. His opening statement?

> I can tell you guys are pretty religious, just look at all the statues of the gods you've got kicking around! You like to cover your bases, too. I noticed you've got an altar marked "to an unknown god." Let me tell you about this God. He's the one-true God of the universe. He made everything, doesn't need you to bring him food, and he doesn't live in a temple.[10]

Paul's experience in Athens was a good reflection of the broader ancient world. Sumerians, Persians, Greeks and everyone else under the sun back then wrote about and worshipped the gods. We've got lots of that writing. The thing is, they had a way of writing about them. We can still read about Greek perspectives on the character of the gods today, many of whom lacked any.

It's the same with the Egyptians, other ancient Near Eastern peoples and later pagan European tribes. None of these gods, as far as we can tell, said and did the sorts of things that Jesus did. Most of them were only interested in power, control, or lots and lots of sex. Sound familiar?

In this world women were commonly treated like objects, and children were considered subhuman. People usually founded their belief of the god's interest in them by how well the crops were doing and how many kids they had. The ancients didn't wonder if the gods loved them. They either found favour with the gods (based on sacrifices, rituals and the like) or they didn't. Love wasn't the issue. People just wanted to keep the gods happy.[11]

Mark's gospel holds two stories, in close proximity to one another, which tell of two occasions when Jesus miraculously fed thousands of people.[12] Mark tells us Jesus was teaching the crowds, but they ran out of food. In both stories he says that Jesus had *compassion* on the crowds. When Jesus looked at people in difficult circumstances, he felt deeply for them, and did something about their situation.

Mark says Jesus was able to take a little food that had been gathered up and turn it into a lot. You may or may not believe in miracles, but the supernatural content of the story isn't what we need to focus on at this moment. The point is: Jesus' first followers believed he was a kind, generous, others-focused person. Jesus loved, practically. The gospels are filled with stories of Jesus' compassion and kindness.

Most gods in ancient mythology demanded something from their worshippers. These kinds of gods took. Jesus gave. His legacy was that he loved people; it was his defining feature.

Bob < Jesus.

When Jesus comes on the scene claiming to be the embodiment of the one-true God of the universe, he bases his teaching on what the Israelite people previously understood God to be like. The Israelites were a small, Semitic tribe who'd had their ups and downs over the centuries. In the grand scheme of ancient political and military history, the Israelites played a minuscule role.[13]

The Israelites did hold to a firm moral and religious code, however. This code was clear on how women and children should be treated, and often differed from the way they were treated in some of the other surrounding cultures.

The Bible says that Jesus was an Israelite, so he grew up learning and practicing this code. We see in the gospels that he didn't objectify women or overlook kids. In fact, he stood up for them on numerous occasions. He treated women and children as whole human beings and welcomed them into his inner circle.

On one occasion Jesus told a child to stand in the middle of a large crowd that had gathered around him and said: *You guys need to be more like this kid.*[14] That's high praise for children, given the Greco-Roman view of them in the first century.

Jesus also invited women to learn alongside men, which was a big no-no in his day and age. He was both morally and ethically progressive for his time, cared for degraded "dispensable" people, and instructed his listeners to reject a low view of human value.

Part of the code the Israelites held to taught, *Don't murder each other.*[15] Jesus took it further. He said, *Don't hate each other.*[16] Jesus knew that murder is hate embodied. Murder is in the heart before it's in the hands. We must deal with the attitude *and* the behaviour, Jesus taught.

Jesus was also said to have hung around and healed lots of sick people, fed the hungry and constantly befriended cultural outcasts. His philanthropic impact on the world certainly puts him in contention of being the most influential human rights activist ever.[17]

Jesus seems like a solid guy, but I know lots of solid guys. I've got friends who feed and clothe the poor and care for the sick too. Some generously donate thousands of dollars year after year to help needy people who live in desperate countries they'll never even visit. There are many wonderful humans hanging around. You and I know lots of them.

Take the time to think of one right now. Who's the best human you know? Write their name on this page if you want. Now, write *Jesus* next to their name. Here, I'll go first:

Bob | Jesus

As awesome as your friend is and as much as you love them, do you think they'll leave a mark on the world the size that Jesus did? Don't get me

WHEN GOD WAS LITTLE

wrong; Bob's great! He spends lots of his time serving at the local hospice. Bob's a good person, but as much as I respect and admire him:

Bob < Jesus

That Jesus was a good person is not what people like to debate and question, even though he was. The questions we ask surround his claims of divinity, as recorded in the gospel accounts. These claims are, as we've noted, a little wacky. Who walks around acting like God himself, even if he *is* super nice?

Jesus didn't eat bacon.

The gospels (Matthew, Mark, Luke and John) tell us Jesus claimed he was God. Unlike lots of ancient literature on the gods, the gospels don't read like mythology. We don't read about Jesus angrily throwing thunderbolts; he's too busy touching lepers, giving sermons, and cleaning mucky feet. No miracle he performed was self-serving.

If the gospels are attempts at mythology, they're poor ones. Compared to the cast of storybook characters we discover buried in antiquity, Jesus makes for one tragically disappointing god.

Over hundreds of years of academic scrutiny, many have shown that the gospels are different from everything else kicking around back then that dealt with supernatural subject matter. The gospels are written like historical documents, or eye-witnessed events, not like folklore.

This is why Jesus is different. This is why he's important. This is why so many people are fascinated and inspired by him. Jesus doesn't look or act like Zeus, yet he claims to be the God who made everything.

What if, you might ask, Jesus is just a part of Jewish lore? The gospel stories could just be an Israelite version of mythology, couldn't they? This is possible, but highly unlikely. Jesus' claims were arguably stranger to the Jewish mind than they were to the Greek one.

First-century Israelites believed, unlike the rest of the Greco-Roman world, that there was only one-true God. No pantheon, no half-gods, just one God. They held firmly that this God had made everything, and was unparalleled in power and majesty.

The Israelites revered this God and called him holy. They believed that seeing God would kill you.[18] Even writing or speaking God's name was risky. His name garnered immense respect. Refusing to adhere to the legislative commands they believed God had given them was, in some cases, punishable by death. Strict rules about creating physical representations (idols) of their Spirit-God were honoured for centuries. *Their deity was not to be made into matter.* [19]

So, when Jesus arrives on the scene saying what he says and doing what he does, it's odd. This would seem to be the *last* place, the *last* culture, the *last* people to produce an individual who thought it plausible he'd be warmly received as *God made of matter.* A guy like that may have done better with a bag of tricks somewhere in Greece a few hundred years earlier.

Considering the first-century Jewish culture Jesus grew up in, his declarations are staggering. It is strange that this man and his teachings grew so popular when we think about where he came from.[20]

But this is what Jesus is said to have claimed: *I'm God in the flesh, and I can prove it.*[21] When you study his life in the gospels, you wonder why people kept inviting him to parties; there must have been something to him. You also wonder how he didn't get himself killed sooner.

That's one big "IF."

Much has changed since the first century. We do share a few things in common with ancient people, however; one of which is the mystifying question of Jesus' true identity. When faced with Jesus' claims, much of the world still says: *Huh? Wasn't he born in a barn? Didn't he die on a cross?*

Jesus is different from the rest of antiquity's mythic personalities and every religious figure before and after him. If his first followers were wrong, as C.S. Lewis famously wrote, Jesus was either a liar or a lunatic.[22] If he was telling the truth, it changes everything. Jesus' claims invite us to scrutinize his story.

What if he was telling the truth?

What if the baby in the hay *was* God?

What does it mean for babies?

What does it mean for hay?

Part Two
Birth Stories

Maybe Christmas, he thought, doesn't come from a store.
Maybe Christmas, perhaps, means a little bit more.
-Dr. Seuss, *How the Grinch Stole Christmas*

Jesus blinked.

In the film *Talladega Nights*, Will Ferrell plays a racing driver named Ricky Bobby. Multiple times in the movie he prays to "baby Jesus":

Dear 8-pound, 6-ounce newborn infant Jesus, don't even know a word yet, just a little infant and so cuddly, but still omnipotent, we just thank you for all the races I've won and the 21.2 million dollars – woo! – love that money, that I have accrued over this past season....Thank you for all your power and your grace, dear baby God. Amen.

When his family tries to remind him that Jesus grew up, Ricky fires back:

Well, I like the Christmas Jesus best and I'm saying grace. When you say grace you can say it to grown-up Jesus, or teenage Jesus, or bearded Jesus, or whoever you want.[23]

You can't blame Ricky. Who doesn't like Christmas Jesus? I find movies about Jesus interesting. How will the filmmaker portray him? What did

Jesus look like? How did he sound? We can learn a lot about our percep-
tions of Jesus from the kinds of films we make about him.

Over the years there's been a wide range of interpretations of
Jesus on screen. Some have noted that in one film made in the seventies, an actor playing Jesus made a creative choice never to blink when
the camera was on him.[24] Apparently, the intent was to create an other-
worldly sense about the character. It's a rather ghostly portrayal of Jesus
and certainly sets him apart from everyone else on screen.

I've seen the movie, and am not so sure about the actor's choice.
Jesus likely blinked just as much as you and me. I'm not absolutely certain, but he probably didn't wander around trying to win endless staring
competitions. He was human.

The first Christian storytellers.

Even though Jesus was human like you and me, he was also clearly special. We know this because of his dramatic historical impact. Jesus' influence caused lots of stories to spread about him, and spread quickly.

When the first Christians saw the immediate impact Jesus was
having, a few of them set out to write his life story down. They wanted to
make sure people understood that Jesus wasn't mythic, or exaggerated.

As Christianity expanded, one of the primary concerns of its
propagators was that early adopters accepted Jesus' human nature. Jesus
was not a vision, nor was he a ghost. Jesus was physically present. He was
real. He blinked.

Even though oral tradition was strong in the ancient world, people
still knew it was important to write things down. As the stories spread,
the first Christians wrote. These writers ended up producing books that
continue to top the world's bestseller lists today—the gospels. Many
famous ancient figures don't have a comprehensive biography. Jesus has
four, and they've lasted:

Matthew
Mark
Luke
John

These men wrote about the life and times of Jesus. Each of them had a different perspective of him (not unlike filmmakers today), and so they told his story in distinctive ways. The gospel writers were researchers and eyewitnesses, living at ground zero.

Matthew

Matthew was one of Jesus' friends and disciples. He was Jewish, so he writes about Jesus from a particularly Jewish perspective. His account of Jesus' birth and infancy begins with telling the reader who Jesus' ancestors were.[25] If we want to get to know someone we usually consider where they've come from. We still do this today (when going on dates or getting to know a new friend) when we ask, "So, what's your family like?"

Matthew quotes the Jewish scriptures a lot. These writings are now commonly known as the Old Testament. He points out that Jesus' life was anticipated long before he came along. Matthew wants his readers to consider that Jesus' arrival was planned. From Matthew's point of view, Jesus is crucial to the Israelites' future because he's rooted in their past.

Mark

Mark was a close friend of both Peter (Jesus' right-hand man) and Paul (arguably Christianity's most important thinker and leader of the first century). Mark was probably the first to write the Jesus story down. Peter's influence in Mark's gospel is heavy. Mark is a shorter work than Matthew, but they share a lot of material. Scholars think Matthew used Mark as a literary source.[26]

Since Mark was the first to write anything down, likely just twenty to thirty years after Jesus lived, his account is quite abbreviated. His goal was to help Jewish people see, even before Matthew came along, that Jesus was something special.

Mark believed that his ancestors anticipated someone like Jesus would turn up one day. He jumped right into his story by quoting one of Israel's most revered prophets who spoke about Jesus' life hundreds of years before his arrival. Mark was making a case for the legitimacy of Jesus' claims.[27]

Luke

Luke was a diligent historian and doctor. He was also friends with, and travelled alongside, both Peter and Paul. He begins by saying he's gone to great pains to make sure all of the details of Jesus' life are accurate:

> Having carefully investigated everything from the beginning, I also have decided to write a careful account for you....so you can be certain of the truth of everything you were taught.[28]

Luke writes with the understanding that Jesus' story was spreading beyond the Jewish community. He depicts Jesus in a way that non-Jewish people would understand. He explained particular cultural details that would be important for non-Jewish people to grasp as they read the story.

The beginning of the book of Luke is sort of like the opening of *Star Wars: A New Hope*[29], with the scrolling yellow text and big John Williams score. Luke tells us about the places and people that matter, grounding Jesus' life in history, and makes mention of the ancient leaders and rulers of Jesus' day. This gives those of us reading today clarity on the time in which Jesus lived.

John

Finally, we have John. Being one of Jesus' best friends, John lived, ate and travelled with him everywhere. He also saw him die, and was emphatic (along with the other three gospel writers) that Jesus came back to life. Though the gospel accounts sometimes differ on timing of events in Jesus' life, and vary in some of the stories they include, each writer is adamant that Jesus literally came back to life.

John probably wrote last, some sixty years after Jesus walked the earth. Some think one of the reasons John may have taken so long to write was because he was digesting it all. He waited till the end of his life, after computing the magnitude of who Jesus was to him, and only then wrote from a seasoned, holistic perspective. John closes his gospel by saying that Jesus did so many incredible things that he couldn't possibly write all of them down.

I once heard a biblical scholar remark, "I relate to John like I relate to my wife. I love it, but I do not claim to [fully] understand it."[30] John's gospel is a poetic, culturally relevant and beautifully constructed piece of literature. It's renowned for its brilliance and mystery, because it's both wonderfully simple and astonishingly deep. It's the first book of the Bible I recommend someone read if they've never read the Bible before.

Charles Dickens opens *A Christmas Carol* with the famous and strange statement: "Marley was dead as a doornail."[31] He goes on to say that it's vital we're sure of this fact or we won't get anything out of story. Two thousand years earlier, John began the tradition of opening Christmas stories with mysterious, poetic and important language:

> In the beginning was the Word, and the Word was with God, and the Word was God. He was in the beginning with God. All things were made through him, and without him was not any thing made that was made. In him was life, and the life was the light of men. The light shines in the darkness, and the darkness has not overcome it.[32]

One of the most curious components of John's gospel is that he doesn't include a birth narrative, at least not a predictable one. His perspective of Jesus' origin is wider. John gives us some *dizzyingly* spectacular views of Jesus. We'll look at some of those later on in part four.

Who cares?

Maybe you're wondering why any of this matters. Because we want to know where to read about Jesus, we need to understand a little about his biographers. This will help us better appreciate his story.

When it comes to detailed narrative surrounding Jesus' infancy, we read Matthew and Luke. Both Mark and John don't speak of Jesus' birth, not because it doesn't matter, but because they're coming at the story from different angles. They're emphasizing different perspectives.

These first Christian writers were adamant that Jesus was both God and human, all at the same time. If any of this is stretching or challenging for you, you're in good company. Welcome to the party!

WHEN GOD WAS LITTLE

Do you know who I am?

Every now and then we hear stories of celebrities or bigwigs asking this question at a restaurant or hotel: "Do you know who I am?" They think they're superior and deserve special treatment. Everyone likes to have his or her ego stroked. Nobody wants to be the rule; we'd rather be the exception.

Deep down, on some level, everyone loves praise, and positive attention. If you've ever accepted an imaginary award in your bathroom mirror, dreamt about walking down a red carpet, or fantasized about your boss gushing over your work performance to your co-workers, you know what I mean.

Nero, a Roman emperor, ruled a few years after Jesus lived. He's famous (or infamous, depending on who you talk to) for his architectural achievements. Nero built a 103-foot bronze statue of himself that sat in his palace courtyard. To put that in perspective, the Statue of Liberty stands at 111 feet tall. Nero's likeness was massive.[33] Nero's palace was so big that ancient graffiti discovered in Rome reads:

> Romans, there's no more room for you, you have to go to [the nearby village of] Veio.[34]

Though Nero built a giant gymnasium and numerous courtyards for Romans to enjoy, he still lived segregated from the masses. One historian writes:

> He was completely isolated in a bubble, and you had to go through a million layers to get to him.[35]

Another notes:

> He wanted to be close to the people, but as their god, not as their friend.[36]

Nero was a man, but he wanted to live like a god. The gospel writers say Jesus was God, but lived like an ordinary man.

Jesus once told his followers not to emulate the religious leaders of their community because they begged for special attention:

30

Beware of the teachers of the law. They like to walk around in flowing robes and love to be greeted with respect in the market-places and have the most important seats in the synagogues and the places of honour at banquets.[37]

According to his biographers, Jesus didn't act like this. He didn't need everyone to tell him he was a big deal, even if he was. His birth narratives show us this quite clearly.

Later on in his biography, Matthew tells us that Jesus asked his friends who the crowds thought he was. This was a question about identity, right in the midst of the miracles, signs and wonders he was preforming. Jesus was extremely popular at this point (as you'd imagine someone who could supernaturally heal sick people would be), and everyone seemed to have a different idea about who he might be.

Then Jesus turned to his friends and asked, "Who do you say I am?"[38] His question is important for a number of reasons. One of them is because it's a very personal question.

Jesus wasn't bothered about a popularity contest, and he didn't seem interested in being made into a local ruler. He wanted people to know who he *really* was. Maybe his birth in a barn holds a couple of clues as to his true nature.

When *Jesus* asked, "Do you know who I am?" He wasn't looking for special treatment. That's clear by how he chose to live. It's clear in how he chose to be born, and later, die.

That last thought is an important one in our journey. For some of us the idea that Jesus *chose* to be born, live and die is a new one. It's an important hinge in understanding Jesus as his first followers knew him.

Spectacular humility.

Matthew's gospel begins with a genealogy. When he recorded Jesus' family line, as you might expect, he included impressive figures from Israel's past: kings, warriors and lots of other important people. Oddly enough, however, he mentions a prostitute and a couple other interesting characters in the list as well.[39] Jesus' background sounds impressive, but what's with all of the regular folk mixed in? What's the point of that?

Some families have estranged uncles or cousins or grandparents, people no one talks about, and perhaps for good reason. Maybe their reputation is less than shimmering. These people get buried, forgotten, ignored. Not so with Jesus. His obscure (even sketchy) relatives are included, actually highlighted by Matthew, to prove a point.

This rhythm of the *spectacular* contrasted with the seemingly *unspectacular* continues in Matthew's version.[40] Jesus' birth is announced by an angel, which is exciting. His mother Mary, however, isn't a queen, movie star or a business tycoon. She's extremely normal, probably a teenager. So is the man she plans to marry. He is, quite literally, a regular Joe.

Once Jesus is born, mysterious magi (or wise men) show up. They've travelled from somewhere in present-day Iran and claim the stars guided them to Bethlehem to see the baby. These astronomers travelled to meet a child, whom they describe as a "king", and to present the family with extravagant and expensive gifts.

Jesus had a bountiful baby shower: gold, and two lavish and pricy spices in frankincense and myrrh. One of those off-road strollers might have been more helpful, however, given the following sequence of events.

Matthew contrasts the swanky baby shower story with an angelic warning to Joseph. He better pack up the family and head to Egypt. A local power-hungry and bloodthirsty ruler named Herod is after the baby. Herod's heard rumours about a new "king" born in the area, and so he orders every male under the age of two to be slaughtered (they always leave that part out in Christmas cards).

Matthew says that God sends an angel to tell Joseph to hit the road. Jesus and his parents become drifters. Travelling to Egypt, Jesus probably learned to speak and walk while living as a refugee.

Notice the contrast. Mysterious and rich astronomers pay homage to a future global superpower in one sequence, who's on the run (or the crawl, rather) in the next.

It's impossible to miss Jesus' humble beginnings. At the same time, it's clear in the narrative that he's important. Jesus seems impressive one moment, and lowly the next. This is one of the reasons people debate about his identity. Shouldn't God be super impressive all of the time?

This trend occurs in the other gospels, too. Thousands flock to hear Jesus' brilliant and captivating teaching, but he doesn't gravitate to the popular or influential in the crowd—he focuses on the kids. At the beginning of one week, Jesus rides into town more popular than a prom king, but is dead on a cross at the end of it.[41] Jesus' importance and power is constantly coupled with his humility.

I remember meeting a famous hockey player at the grocery store when I was a kid, and he signed an autograph for me. I used to take it out and look at it all the time. When extraordinary people choose to humble themselves to associate with or help us, it inspires us. Deep down, we each suspect that everyone puts his or her hockey pants on one leg at a time.

Today, this attracts people to Jesus. Nobody likes a show-off, and we lose respect for famous people when they demand special attention. When a great person is humble we love them for it. Humility has become a positive trait in Western culture. So, when people act arrogantly or show off, we generally turn our noses up at them.[42]

This wasn't the case in Jesus' day. Back then famous or powerful people wanted to stand out and rise above the riff-raff. They'd throw extravagant parties or give expensive gifts just to prove how rich they were. Powerful people would parade their notoriety. Every move was a political ploy to remind the world of how important they were. Like building a 103-foot statue of yourself, for example.

Humility as we know it now wasn't a respected quality in Jesus' time. Powerful people were *expected* to look and act powerful. If they didn't, they'd inevitably lose their power. Researchers have recently shown that Jesus' life was a significant turning point in Western history. Because of Jesus, humility moved from being a negative trait to a positive one.[43]

Greatness didn't spring from having to remind everyone you were great, post-Jesus. We'll talk about greatness and humility further in part six.

Misery loves company.

The first Christians were clear about Jesus' divinity *and* his humanity. Ricky Bobby got something right. Jesus was a real, live infant.

If Jesus was human, just like you and me, then we can infer a number of things about his birth and infancy: Jesus likely cried, breastfed, and even wet himself. Have you ever thought about that? Jesus needed his parents to feed him, clothe him, and buy the diapers. In other words, he was vulnerable.

WHEN GOD WAS LITTLE

I love visiting the hospital when my friends have kids. There's nothing like holding a fresh baby. Some of them are little, some of them are on the larger side (poor mom), and some of them look kind of funny. No matter how they look, however, one thing they all feel is fragile.

The dependency a new baby has on its caregivers is overwhelming. I've seen the looks in my friends' eyes when they hold their first child. They look different than they did the week before. I went to church as a kid. We used to this song in Sunday school:

He's got the whole world in his hands.
He's got the whole wide-world in his hands.
He's got the whole world in his hands.[44]

Mary and Joseph probably didn't feel any different than new parents do today. They must have held their new baby, in the midst of all the strange events surrounding his birth, and still felt the weight of responsibility and awe. *He* was in *their* hands. Jesus needed taking care of. If any of this sounds sacrilegious, listen to Peter (one of Jesus' closest friends) and consider what he thought about him.

Peter lived, ate, and travelled with Jesus, probably for about three years. The gospels tell us all about him. We have a couple of letters written by him in the Bible's New Testament, too. One of Peter's letters was written to a group of people going through a particularly rough time. They were being thrown into prison, beat up and even burned alive because of their beliefs about Jesus.

In the middle of all this, Peter reminded them that Jesus had dealt with hardship and suffering just like they did. Jesus had graduated from the school of hard-knocks, and Peter and his friends were enrolled in the very same program.

Dear friends, don't be surprised at the fiery trials you are going through, as if something strange were happening to you. Instead, be very glad—for these trials make you partners with Christ in his suffering...[45]

Peter knew firsthand that Jesus lived like a regular person, and suffered in life, just like everyone else. If Peter's friends suffered, they could take

34

comfort in the fact that Jesus had struggled, bled and experienced how brutal life can be as well.

The simple fact that Jesus understood their struggles was comforting to Peter's friends. The first Christians believed that Jesus knew what pain, loss, heartache and discouragement felt like. He wasn't immune to everything the world could throw at a person.

If Jesus was just a great teacher, or simply an exemplary social activist, this might bring some encouragement. Misery loves company. When inspiring figures experience trouble we feel a kinship with them. We remember that we're all in the same boat.

A couple of years ago a famous actress tripped over her dress while climbing the stairs to receive her *Best Actress* Oscar at the Academy Awards. She embraced the moment, didn't take herself too seriously, and everybody loved her for it. Now whenever we stumble up or down the stairs in public, we can say to ourselves, "Hey, I'm just like Jennifer Lawrence!"

To the first Christians, Jesus was more than a celebrity, great teacher, or fantastic moral example. They actually thought Jesus was God with a capital G. So, when Peter reminds the young Christians that God with a capital G had walked more than a mile in their shoes, they were comforted.

The one-true God of the universe, whom Peter and his friends held in staggeringly high regard, wasn't disconnected from, or disinterested in, regular life. The first Christians believed God had pulled on their skin, lived amongst them, and knew their plight. This God, demonstrated in Jesus, could identify with them, and they with him. *Jesus has been there, don't forget that*, said Peter.

Imagine that. A God who gets it.

One barn, please.

The first Christians believed Jesus did everything he did willingly, not begrudgingly.[46] Millions around the world would love this luxury. I don't recall choosing much as an infant. If Jesus was God, then God chose to be born in a barn. He chose a life of vulnerability and trouble. What does that say about him?

Nativity sets are those little wooden scenes religious folk put on their mantelpieces at Christmas. There's usually a few figurines in them: a Mary, a Joseph, some shepherds, and maybe a few wise men. Toss in a couple of farm animals, some hay, and maybe an angel straddling the roof, and you've got yourself a decent Christmas tableau.

In actuality, the stable Jesus was born in was probably more cave-like. At best it was the animal room in someone's house. Back then, people would designate rooms in their homes to house livestock. There, the animals could be safe and fed.[47]

Have you ever rented a hotel or motel room only to walk inside and realize it's not what you expected? Maybe it was dirty or smelled like smoke. Maybe it faced the parking lot when you thought it would face the beach.

When Mary and Joseph couldn't get a room in Bethlehem, they ended up laying the newborn baby Jesus in a feeding trough (or manger). This meant they had to bed down with the animals. There was no room for Jesus amongst the humans of Bethlehem.[48] The first noises and smells baby Jesus experienced emanated from animals. His bed frame was a bowl and his mattress was hay. No one brought baby Jesus a stuffed animal, or an "IT'S A BOY!" helium balloon the day he was born (the wise men probably showed up a year or so later).

The gospel writers tell us Jesus wasn't accidentally allotted to sleep in a grimy motel room. Nobody mixed up the reservation booking. His family slept in the equivalent of a motel parking lot. Astonishingly, we're lead to believe this was the plan all along.

Jesus developed in utero and pushed through the birth canal. He slept his first night in an animal trough, and became a political refugee before he turned three.

Once we start thinking about the stable, and the hay, and baby Jesus on the lam from nasty old King Herod, we begin to experience the wonder of the Christmas story. Visions of a distant, unfeeling, tyrannical God subside, and a new vision of an intentional, relatable, humble Jesus begins to inform our perspective of the divine.

Part Three
First Impressions

Buddy the Elf! What's your favourite colour?!
-Buddy, *Elf*

Nice to meet you.

It might be wrong to judge a book by its cover, but you can certainly learn a thing or two about it based on how said book first strikes you.

I remember meeting one of my best friends for the first time in a dormitory hallway. Our rooms were adjacent, and one day we emerged from them simultaneously. We each said hi and asked where the other was from. Because we were insecure nineteen-year-olds, we also each tried to *out-cool* the other.

I remember thinking he was stuck up. He remembers thinking I was kind of grumpy, but had sweet surfer hair. Our first impressions of one another were accurate. He *was* a little proud, and I'm *still* a little grumpy. Sadly, I've since lost the frosted tips.

Our first impressions of one another took some time to get over. It wasn't until later in September that we finally connected during a game of soccer. Our friendship's been strong ever since.

First impressions matter. They affect how we relate to one another and can bring two people together, or drive them apart. What's our first impression of Jesus?

Representing the family.

Preparing for formal functions or weddings in my teenage years was a dramatic struggle. It was the same every time: I would dress how I liked, come downstairs, and inevitably face my mother's disapproving gaze. I'd be told to go back to my room and try again. Even though I knew I'd have to change, I never stopped trying.

My struggle for individuality (and comfort, quite honestly; I only wear a suit when I absolutely have to) continued wedding after wedding. My parents' words are forever etched in my mind: "When you leave *this* house you are representing *this* family." This meant I better think carefully about which outfit I put on next.

The mantra didn't mean I was forced to dress posh every day of my adolescent life. Clothing wasn't the issue. This was a broader philosophy my parents wisely instilled. It meant I was expected to be polite, thoughtful and generally well-mannered everywhere I went. I was their child, and carried their character. In healthy doses this is appropriate. We pass on the values we believe matter. So, when it came to attending a formal event, I was expected to dress and act appropriately. Fair enough! Sorry, teenage me, you lose.

How we dress, act and speak says a lot about who we are. This doesn't mean we're a *better* person depending on how courteous we are or how nice we scrub up. It just means that appearance, actions and speech are windows into our background, value system and worldview.

John's gospel says that Jesus was God's *Word*.[49] We'll consider this in more detail in part four, but for now let's simply note this: John believed that when God spoke, we met Jesus. For John, Jesus was the language and logic of God,[50] and expressed his heart and character while he lived amongst us.[51]

This is why our first impression of Jesus is vital. Jesus could have shown up as a fully-grown man, having teleported from some heavenly realm. He could have immediately jumped into his work on earth, focused on efficiency, and streamlined his mission on Google calendar. This isn't his narrative, however. Our first glimpse of Jesus is of an infant lying in a manger.

EE-man-u-el (what's in a name?)

There's a family in my church who names their kids a little differently. They have names like: *Hope, Mercy, and Justice*—you get the picture. Naming their children this way obviously reflects the parents' values and passions. They hope the name will help define the child as she or he grows up.

Matthew tells us that Joseph and Mary were instructed by an angel to call their new baby "Jesus."[52] Jesus means *God saves*. He also says a Jewish prophet named Isaiah, who lived seven hundred years before Jesus, predicted this:

> Behold, the virgin shall conceive and bear a son, and they shall call his name Immanuel.[53]

Immanuel means *God with us*. Names in the ancient world were of great importance. Jesus' name is crucial in understanding who he is. Matthew begins by telling us that Jesus' name means *God is with us, and he saves*.

As we noted in part two, Jesus experienced life like we do. I recently heard a fellow pastor make a simple yet profound insight. He was talking about how important it is for Christians to simply love people, just because. This way of life, he said, is at the core of the Christian message, so it must be the Christian medium. He based his thinking on Jesus' life and noted that Jesus was quite content to live amongst us for thirty years before he started teaching, preaching and healing. Jesus was just *with* us, period. Jesus was happy to feel what we feel, and live how we live. He didn't rush things; he wasn't in a hurry.[54]

The gospels tell us Jesus' arrival was so under the radar that when he started working miracles and teaching thousands, many rejected him, even though they were amazed at what he did and said. Mark says Jesus was rejected outright in his hometown because they felt he couldn't be anything special based on their familiarity with his humble origins. Wasn't he Mary and Joseph's boy? What makes him so special?[55]

Back to my parent's mantra: *When you leave this house you represent this family.* The first Christians believed that when Jesus left his heavenly standing, he was representing who God was and how God operates. Perhaps God could put on a big show, but does that mean he always does? Maybe he acts differently than we might expect, they thought.

This is why Christians care so much about who Jesus is. If he's God with us, then his life, words and actions give us unique insight into the Maker of all things. This is why the thought of Jesus brings so many such comfort. This is also why Christians should be people who bring comfort to others.

Recently, an elderly man in my church died. He had cancer and lived only a couple of months after the diagnosis. When I called him at home to see if he'd like me to come visit, he hesitated. He explained that he was tired because he'd had so many visitors and friends come from the church to care for him. He literally felt *over-supported* by his church family.

Eventually, I visited him. We talked about life, and death and if he was scared of what might come next. He said he wasn't, and that he trusted God with his future. I could tell he was at peace, felt loved and was determined to finish life well. He drew all this from his relationship with God, his family and his friends from church.

I know a lot of people who walk through horrible circumstances, and yet carry deep peace and joy. Many of them would tell you this comes from their trust in God's faithfulness to be with them through thick and thin, and the example of this kind of faithfulness by their Christian community.

The Psalms are a collection of poems and songs found in the Bible. One of my favourites says this:

> The LORD is near to the broken-hearted and saves the crushed
> in spirit.[56]

The Bible teaches that through Jesus, God was near and God saved. It also teaches that God is still doing this today.

Who's on the guest list?

As was his custom, grown-up Jesus attended lots of social functions. Once, at a party, he noticed other guests jostling for the best seats at the table. Later, he turned to the host and said:

> When you give a dinner or a banquet, do not invite your friends

or your brothers or your relatives or rich neighbours, lest they also invite you in return and you be repaid. But when you give a feast, invite the poor, the crippled, the lame, the blind, and you will be blessed, because they cannot repay you. For you will be repaid at the resurrection of the just.[57]

Jesus encouraged his followers to be open to everyone. He sought out the down and out, marginalized and unimpressive individuals; the people who can't pay you back.

Christmas, according to the gospels, shows us that Jesus' life both inaugurated and modelled this philosophy. Grown-up Jesus walked the walk. Baby Jesus crawled the crawl.

We've already mentioned several members of the cast of Christmas. Mary, Joseph, the wise men. Who else was on the guest list for the *Welcome to earth, Almighty God* party?

Shepherds, dirt, angels and fear.

Have you ever visited a friend in hospital who's recently had a baby and arrived a little too early, beating grandparents, uncles and aunts there? It's awkward. You tend to wonder if you should even be there at all, and are tempted to cut the visit short. Aren't you imposing? Surely more important people should hold the baby first.

The shepherds might have felt this way when they turned up the night Jesus was born. Luke's gospel tells us they were working in the nearby fields of a small town called Bethlehem. The story goes that some angels appeared to them, and put on quite a show:

> And in the same region there were shepherds out in the field, keeping watch over their flock by night. And an angel of the Lord appeared to them, and the glory of the Lord shone around them, and they were filled with great fear. And the angel said to them, "Fear not, for behold, I bring you good news of great joy that will be for all the people. For unto you is born this day in the city of David a Saviour, who is Christ the Lord. And this will be a sign for you: you will find a baby wrapped in swaddling cloths and lying

in a manger." And suddenly there was with the angel a multitude
of the heavenly host praising God and saying,

"Glory to God in the highest, and on earth peace among those
with whom he is pleased!"

When the angels went away from them into heaven, the shepherds said to one another, "Let us go over to Bethlehem and see
this thing that has happened, which the Lord has made known to
us." And they went with haste and found Mary and Joseph, and
the baby lying in a manger.[58]

The angel scene might feel a tad Spielberg-ian, even grandiose. The
celestial chorus line, however, wasn't delivering a message to royalty, a
wealthy family or even an overly religious bunch. These were shepherds.
The tradition of contrast in the Christmas story continues.

Many people's view of shepherds is sterile and cute. We might
picture children wearing bathrobes in church Christmas plays or decora-
tive figurines on mantelpieces. In Jesus' day, however, shepherds were
anything but sterile, and nobody found them adorable.

Shepherds lived with their sheep in fields on the outskirts of
towns and villages. They were nomadic by trade, of lower class, and
had a nasty reputation for thievery. Shepherds also weren't permitted
to give testimony in Jewish law courts because people thought them to
be untrustworthy. Shepherds were outsiders, and were even considered
ritually "unclean" by their own religious system.[59] Shepherds were dirty.

Luke records that as this rag-tag band of misfits worked that night,
an angel showed up and starting speaking to them.

Now, not to say that a luminous angelic vision wouldn't impress us
today, but can you imagine what it must have been like for first century
sheepherders living in a time without electricity, movie theatres and rock
concerts? There you are looking after your sheep in the dead of night,
maybe dozing off a little, and then—WHAM—someone throws a switch,
and a massive gang of radiant, celestial beings light up the night sky. It
must have been mind-blowing. No wonder Luke describes them as "terri-
fied."

Notice what the angel says, however: "Fear not, for behold, I bring
you good news of great joy that will be for all the people." These first

words to the shepherds, "Fear not," are actually found all over the Bible. One writer notes:

> Do you know what the most frequent command in the Bible turns out to be? What instruction, what order is given, again and again, by God, by angels, by Jesus, by prophets and apostles? What do you think—"Be good"? "Be holy, for I am holy"? Or negatively, "Don't sin"? "Don't be immoral"? No. The most frequent command in the Bible is: *"Don't be afraid." Don't be afraid. Fear not. Don't be afraid.*[60]

The angel echoes an ancient and faithful message from God to humankind: *You've got nothing to be afraid of.* After "Fear not" the next words from the angel concern "good news of great joy." According to the angel, Jesus' arrival is *good news.* Good news is actually what *gospel* means.

The shepherds of Bethlehem were the first to visit newborn Jesus. Weren't they imposing? Apparently not. They got a special and spectacular invitation. If God's plan was unfolding as intended, then the angels didn't deliver the invite to the wrong address. The shepherds *belonged* in the barn. They got the first impression.

Luke tells us that the shepherds rushed over to find the newborn baby Jesus. I wonder if any of the shepherds held him. Did they get their shepherd-stink on him? If Jesus was God, then God didn't mind the company of dirty shepherds. He welcomed them.

Next, Luke says the shepherds left the baby, Mary and Joseph, and told everyone they met what had happened. This part makes me chuckle. The irony is delicious. If God's intention upon arrival was to begin a legitimate global movement, surely he could have selected more respectable messengers than shepherds, couldn't he?

> And all who heard it wondered at what the shepherds told them.[61]

Notice that Luke doesn't say, *And all who heard it immediately believed the shepherds, started going to church, and ran out to purchase "Baby Jesus is my Homeboy" t-shirts, because everyone knows shepherds are trustworthy and upstanding citizens.*

People wondered at the events because they were spectacular,

WHEN GOD WAS LITTLE

but also perhaps it was because this news was being relayed to them by a bunch of smelly sheepherders. Maybe God was making a point when he planned out the guest list. Maybe the outsiders weren't outsiders any longer.

Our first impression of Jesus isn't that he's proud, removed, or even sterile! He's humble, present, and approachable.

What does Jesus' first impression say?

Don't be afraid.
I'm not afraid of your dirt.
There's good news for everyone.

Part Four
Intergalactic Infant

He's only a kid, Harry. We can take him.
-Marv, *Home Alone*

Bad wedding presents.

Friends of mine got married about ten years ago. Amidst the many gifts they received were a couple of less desirable acquisitions. Not everyone uses the registry. If you've ever gotten married you can probably relate.

My favourite present was the most chilling picture of Jesus I've ever laid eyes on, a painting in a thick gold frame. A Mediterranean town was in the background, with Jesus in the foreground. His arms were open wide to the viewer. This Jesus boasted a unique gaze, a stare that made the hair on the back of your neck stand on end. It appeared the artist wished to capture that rarely seen side of Jesus that would terrify small children. I told my newlywed friends they should hang the piece above their bed. Its actual home became a closet, until they re-gifted it.

Over the years it's been passed from couple to couple as a sort of gag wedding gift. Amongst the toasters and crockpots, many a gift table has been laden with a familiar large, square shape. Though elegantly wrapped, everyone knows what lies beneath the paper: death-stare Jesus.

Perhaps the artist was trying to capture the same sentiment as the makers of that seventies Jesus movie I mentioned earlier: an other-worldly Jesus. You can't blame an artist for trying. If Jesus was more than human, how does one convey that?

WHEN GOD WAS LITTLE

That's one big baby.

I love nature. One of the things I love most about nature is how awe-inspiring and vast it is. The mountains are huge, and the ocean is almost unfathomably powerful. Trees that are hundreds of years old leave me breathless. Living around Vancouver, Canada, that's just my backyard.

When I think about the rest of the province, or the country, and then the world, I get overwhelmed. The earth is huge! Then I start thinking about our solar system, the sun, the moon, the other planets, and the stars. In my monthly subscription to *National Geographic* I read about the seemingly infinite expanse of outer space. These thoughts leave me adrift in awe. We're tiny, you and I, aren't we?

I resonate with one biblical poet who wrote:

> When I look at your heavens, the work of your fingers, the moon and the stars, which you have set in place, what is man that you are mindful of him, and the son of man that you care for him?[62]

I recently sat next to an interesting man on a five-hour flight. I don't know about you, but when I fly I hope to either be seated next to someone who wants to sleep, or at least someone fascinating. I was in for a treat when this guy sat down next to me.

I'm never sure how strangers will act around me once I share that I'm a pastor. I've become accustomed to asking people on planes as many questions as possible before they have a chance to ask me what my job is. It's a tricky little strategy, but so far it's paid off. I got tons out of the guy in the seat next to me before I had to tell him I was a religious nut.

Turned out my new friend was an astronomer. I'm fascinated by space, so I tried to maintain some composure and not get too giddy. I had a thousand questions.

He told me he spent most of his time teaching, but in past years he was what you'd call a *planet hunter*. He helped discover a couple of planetary disks beyond our solar system, saying they were "young, infants really, still in their swaddling clothes" (by this point he had learned I was a minister, so he threw in some biblical Christmas language for me). We exchanged business cards, and he said if I was ever in his neck of the woods he'd gladly give me a tour of his department at the university.

Serendipitously, the magazine I had packed in my carry-on boasted a cover that read: *Is anybody out there? Life beyond earth.* He chuckled when I showed him my in-flight reading material, and understood why I nerded out once he revealed what he did for a living. I took a photo of him holding the magazine and encouraged him to sign up for Instagram and Twitter, saying he'd be my new favourite follow if he started posting photos. I'd love to see what he and his colleagues spy through big, expensive telescopes.

It's easy to forget, but conversations with people like my astronomer friend remind us that the universe is a big place. It's almost too big for us to fathom. This guy and his friends are in awe of what they study. They've got thousands of questions, too. After years and years of schooling and research, he still lit up when he shared about the vastness and complexity of the cosmos.

The biblical story says God created all that vastness, the entire universe.[63] A being with that kind of power and creative juice has inspired and intrigued philosophers, artists, and scientists since humans started scribbling on walls. A God that big, the Bible says, visited us in the person of Jesus.

Sometimes people say things like, "God is bigger than your problems." I think they hope it will encourage others to trust that God is in control, and can handle their issues. They're well-intentioned.

But God's bigness and ability to handle what I can throw at him isn't my primary concern. If the God of the Bible is out there, of course he's huge and powerful. My primary concern is not *if* God can handle my problems, it's if God *cares* about my problems at all.

This is what's staggering about Jesus' humble beginnings, and earthly life and times. If he's more than human, if he's the one-true God of the universe, star smith and planet former, what's he doing in the hay? Does it have anything to do with me?

Does Jesus really = God?

The author of the biblical book of Hebrews held Jesus in high regard. They weighed the evidence, pulled apart the puzzle, and tried to wrap their heads around a cosmic Jesus.

Hebrews starts like this:

WHEN GOD WAS LITTLE

> Long ago, at many times and in many ways, God spoke to our
> fathers by the prophets, but in these last days he has spoken to
> us by his Son, whom he appointed the heir of all things, through
> whom also he created the world. He is the radiance of the glory
> of God and the exact imprint of his nature, and he upholds the
> universe by the word of his power.[64]

The author of Hebrews identifies Jesus as God's Son, but a different kind
of son than the demi-gods of Greek mythology we mentioned in part one.
They tell us that Jesus was the person *through whom* the world was created. Hebrews says Jesus holds the universe together.

Paul made a similar statement about Jesus in another biblical book
written to a group of people called the Colossians:

> He is the image of the invisible God, the firstborn of all creation.
> For by him all things were created, in heaven and on earth, vis-
> ible and invisible, whether thrones or dominions or rulers or
> authorities—all things were created through him and for him.
> And he is before all things, and in him all things hold together.[65]

Notice how many books in the Bible's New Testament begin with the
assertion that Jesus is a big deal. He's not God's sidekick, he's not just a
prophet, he's not an angel. To the first Christians he was God. Made of the
same matter or substance. He's been around from the beginning, and he
keeps the universe running.

Jesus did and said things no one else had ever done or said, or has
since, for that matter. The first Christians couldn't shake this. When they
surveyed their religious past they saw that Jesus was the embodiment of
dozens of prophecies handed down to them from generations past.

Paul spent years trying to stamp the message of Jesus out before
he became one of Christianity's most important figures. One day he saw
something he couldn't explain. More accurately, he saw *someone.*

The book of Acts tells us Paul had a vision of Jesus that changed his
life. This moment was so eye-opening (pun intended, read Acts 9) that
it forced Paul to radically alter his entire world view and belief system.
Some argue he was one of the most trained and learned religious men in
the Jewish world at the time. He was also a venomous persecutor of Jesus' first followers.[66] After his eye-opening experience, he had to re-think

52

everything he thought he knew. For Paul and thousands of Jesus' other contemporaries, Jesus = God.

Jesus, the Father, and the Spirit.

The New Testament, along with the rest of the Bible, leads its subscribers to believe that God is *Triune*. This is a fancy word for *three in one*. God the Father, God the Son, and God the Spirit. The God of the Bible is one being, but three distinct persons.

This is a challenging thought. Many feel this concept of God's personhood is illogical, even silly. But the Bible is a collection of human-kind's interaction with this God, and a Triune deity is prominent through-out the book. A comprehensive survey of the biblical story strongly asserts that God is three *and* one.

Let's consider, however, that if we're entertaining the thought of an all-powerful, omnipresent and omniscient being logically, perhaps we would be wise not to scoff at the possibility that its nature may be a little challenging to compute. Is it really beyond the realm of possibility?

The first Christians believed Jesus to be fully human, but also fully God. In studying the Bible we find that Jesus is a member of what is called the *Trinity*, along with the Father and the Spirit.[67] This is why books like Hebrews and Colossians start like they do. To these writers, there was more to the grungy, rabbi Jesus than met the eye.

When God speaks.

This might be slightly new for some of us, but let's do a little biblical study. Think of it like investigating any other form of literature.

In part two we briefly looked at John's gospel and noticed how he opens his biography of Jesus:

> In the beginning was the Word, and the Word was with God, and the Word was God. He was in the beginning with God. All things were made through him, and without him was not any thing made that was made. In him was life, and the life was the light of men. The light shines in the darkness, and the darkness has not overcome it.[68]

Notice the first three words, "in the beginning." John uses these words intentionally. They're meant to trigger a thought in the mind of the reader: *Hey, I've heard that before!* The first book of the Jewish scriptures is Genesis. It starts this way:

> In the beginning, God created the heavens and the earth. The earth was without form and void, and darkness was over the face of the deep. And the Spirit of God was hovering over the face of the waters. And God said, "Let there be light," and there was light.[69]

John's working about a dozen literary wonders in the first words of his gospel (you'd need to be able to read ancient Greek to notice them), but right away, us regular folk can spot a couple of key similar elements:

God and his Word in the beginning.
God speaking.
Light and darkness.

God *speaks* creation into existence in Genesis (Jesus being the agent of that generative work), and God's *Word* is revealed most clearly in the person of Jesus, God-made-flesh.

Light imagery is very important in John's gospel. He says Jesus is *the light and the life*. He means that Jesus is the origin of both of these things. Jesus is the light and life giver. Genesis says God's first creative burst came when he said, "let there be light." Light is created by God's word and John identifies Jesus as this *Word*. Later in John's gospel, Jesus calls himself the "light of the world."[70]

John can get deep, fast. For now, what we should notice is that he and the other first Christians were absolutely convinced that Jesus was not just a man. Jesus was the one-true God of the universe as previously understood throughout Jewish history.

When we talk about baby Jesus (according to John), we're talking about an Intergalactic Infant. John calls Jesus "the Word" of God. This Word has power, is a person, and "the Word became flesh and dwelt among us..."[71] As we said earlier: *when God speaks, we meet Jesus.*

Jesus was both nothing (and something) to write home about.

It's plausible that writing like John's could come along a couple genera-tions after Jesus was kicking around. Perhaps some passionate poet, romanticizing and exaggerating a man he never met could have turned Jesus into a God he never was. But these words don't come from an es-tranged individual with an overactive imagination. They come from John, a man who knew how ordinary Jesus was in many ways.

John was probably the closest friend Jesus had. He sat with Jesus at the last meal he ate, and watched him die on a cross.[72] He also said he was the first to investigate the empty tomb Jesus supposedly resurrected from.[73] John's gospel is staunchly different from the other gospels. Some scholars believe this is the case *because* John was Jesus' closest disciple.[74]

These scholars assert that a rabbi's (or teacher's) closest disciple had a special role. Knowing and understanding the rabbi the best, they were supposed to pass on and correctly apply the teacher's lessons to a wider audience. John was closest to the heart of Jesus and was part of the inner circle that knew him best. His goal was to help the world, not just the Jewish people, understand who Jesus really was.

When John writes about Jesus you might think he would spend time emphasizing Jesus' humanity. Maybe he would regale us with intimate moments and stories that only a best friend could relate. Some of these are present in his gospel, but John also spends loads of time emphasizing Jesus' divine nature.

John implores his audience to correctly identify Jesus as the one-true God of the universe. He does this in other biblical books, as well as in the last book of the Bible, Revelation. John's vision of Jesus is dazzling:

No one who denies the Son has the Father. Whoever confesses the Son has the Father also. Let what you heard from the begin-ning abide in you. If what you heard from the beginning abides in you, then you too will abide in the Son and in the Father.[75]

In Revelation John writes about the visions of Jesus he had later in life. These visions were so vivid he had to describe them using rich imagery and metaphor. In the first chapter he describes seeing Jesus:

When I saw him, I fell at his feet as though dead. But he laid his right hand on me, saying, "Fear not, I am the first and the last, and the living one. I died, and behold I am alive forevermore, and I have the keys of Death and Hades. Write therefore the things that you have seen, those that are and those that are to take place after this."[76]

Is the dazzling image John paints of Jesus a far cry from the friend he shared meals with? Perhaps John experienced a Jesus who was simultaneously humble *and* awe-inspiring. John's vision of Jesus isn't overly chummy, nor is it inaccessibly exalted. John believed humans could be friends with this gloriously magnificent Jesus. It's a perfect balance.

Might this say something about Jesus' true nature? Doesn't the fact that his closest friend was so utterly convinced that Jesus was otherworldly, yet incredibly near, rather compelling?

John knew Jesus for a maximum of three years. The two probably met when John was still a teenager. He spent less time with Jesus than you and I did in high school.

Imagine the impact Jesus must have made on him. John spent the rest of his *entire life* telling others about Jesus. Christian tradition holds that John lived a long life, eventually ending up an old man imprisoned on an island called Patmos because his story was threatening the stability of the Roman Empire. The first Christians held bold convictions about Jesus that changed the world forever. They believed Jesus to be glorious and exalted. They also believed he was humble and accessible.

Adventures in accessibility.

Every year our church holds a Christmas play that stars children of all ages. A Sunday is dedicated to learning the true meaning of Christmas through dramatic art and music as performed by the kids.

Over the years this production has grown, become wonderfully rambunctious, and our church has learned to expect the unexpected. One year, during a musical number, I was lowered through the roof in a gorilla costume. You might wonder what that has to do with Christmas. It was a stretch, but we made it work.

Some of my fondest memories of the kid's play are from the first ones I was a part of. Most Christmas plays incorporate some sort of a nativity scene, and ours were no different. We had a manger, a baby Jesus, a Mary and a Joseph, shepherds, wise men, donkeys...even the odd Christmas gorilla.

One year a young boy (who we'll call Tim) was chosen to play a wise man. Tim was physically and mentally challenged. He was also hearing impaired and used a wheelchair. He was extremely mischievous and a lot of fun.

Tim and I spent a lot of time together back then. I'd pick him up once a week to give his foster parents a breather, and we'd just hang out. We'd go for walks, eat McDonalds and wander toy stores. Tim also had a way with the ladies. One year I took him to camp for a week and noticed he had a particular knack for getting girls to push him around in his wheelchair. He was perfectly capable of wheeling himself, but where was the fun in that?

When it came time for Tim's big role as a wise man, I was the obvious choice to help him down the aisle with the gift he was supposed to present to baby Jesus. The morning promised to be interesting.

The big moment came, so Tim donned his crown and cape. He rolled into the auditorium, gift in lap, and wheeled down the aisle. Once he got to the front, we lifted his chair onto the stage. He delivered his gift (*delivered* being a generous term, it was really more of a toss), and took his spot with the other wise men. That was that. Except it wasn't.

During the final musical montage, Tim began a number of attempts to steal all of baby Jesus' gifts. It was cute, so we let him have his fun. His cheeky smile and warm heart helped him get away with a lot back then.

Things had to be put to a stop, however, when Tim moved beyond petty larceny and began poking baby Jesus with his wise man's sceptre. A plastic doll played the Christ child that year, thankfully. No infants were harmed in the making of this Christmas play. Someone eventually took charge, and Tim's mischief came to an end. One might find the entire sequence of events horribly sacrilegious, if it wasn't so funny.

Why do we find moments like these amusing? Why do we allow them to happen in the first place? If Jesus really is Almighty God in the flesh, maker of heaven and earth, shouldn't we keep the irreverent, frankincense-thieving Tims of this world miles away from him? Doesn't Jesus deserve more respect than that?

Jesus might have deserved respect, but he never demanded it at the expense of people who wanted to be near him. Tim, and anyone else who wanted to, got to take a closer look. Even though Jesus was precious, he didn't act like it. Perhaps he was born in a barn and laid in a manger so as to be absolutely accessible to everyone.

Divine fine china.

As we noted earlier, nativity sets, though thought-provoking and cute, aren't always an accurate representation of what Jesus' birth really looked like. Some of them are simple and humble. Others are fancy, with beautifully decorated figurines in unrealistic poses. I don't *really* care what a nativity set looks like, but I do find the perfectly pristine ones a little odd. Sometimes they're so clean, groomed and genteel that baby Jesus is simply replaced by a shape. God incarnate is represented by, and relegated to, a bit of shiny marble.

Some people treat God like a kind of divine fine china. They think they have to handle him with great care, only removing him from the fancy cabinet on special occasions. Jesus' birth, life and death tell us that God belongs in the everyday, however. The first Christians thought Jesus was *the* cosmic superpower. They also witnessed him living amongst us, eating with us, and sleeping under the stars from time to time.

Maybe God isn't as precious as porcelain. Maybe he doesn't need to be handled with care or approached with caution. This isn't to say God shouldn't be respected, or honoured. The first Christians were able to deeply respect and worship God, but they couldn't deny his humble character as seen in Jesus, either.

My friend Doug likes to say that "God got messy," when he talks about Jesus. Perhaps God isn't divine fine china. Maybe Jesus' birth in a barn was an invitation to all of us to take a closer look, even if it meant he would be poked and prodded.

What if God's not only bigger than our problems, but also willing to—even desperate to—come down to our level, live amongst us and do something about them?

Part Five
Never Break Character

Hobo: "What exactly is...is your persuasion on the Big Man, since you brought him up?"
The Boy: "Well, I... I want to believe... but..."
Hobo: "But you don't want to be bamboozled. You don't want to be led down the primrose path! You don't want to be conned or duped. Have the wool pulled over your eyes. Hoodwinked! You don't want to be taken for a ride. Railroaded!"
-*The Polar Express*

Commit to the bit.

I love a good laugh. I'll also shamelessly admit I love a good cry. Christmas movies (or even commercials) have been known to make me shed a tear or two. There's something about the stories we tell at Christmas time: reconciliation, generosity, hope. They strike a chord.

Great comedy and great drama share a number of things in common. One of them is commitment. When someone commits to a character, that character (and the story they're telling) becomes believable. Even when bits or sketches are absurd, a committed comic or actor entertains us because they're all the more determined to deliver an outlandish character and story.

Actors like Will Ferrell and Daniel Day Lewis are known for their commitment. I recently saw an interview wherein an actor shared an embarrassing story. While collaborating on a movie, he thought losing some clothing at a particular moment might ramp up the humour in a scene.

When the time came to shoot the scene, however, he wavered. The film's director thought the original idea was funny and wanted to use it, so he challenged the actor by telling him, "Will Ferrell would do it." The actor begrudgingly stripped down.[77]

Never breaking character is important because dramatic and comedic actors alike are shooting for the same goal: believability. An actor should make us believe they *are* the character. One moment of inconsistency can ruin the audience's whole experience. When a character is funny, we laugh. When a character is scary, we hide beneath blankets on the couch. Heath Ledger's performance as the Joker in *The Dark Knight*[78] is unnerving and frightening because he played a psychotic and unpredictable character, and pulled it off brilliantly.

Part of good acting is about thoroughly knowing and committing to your character. Part of producing a great overall performance is consistently committing to said character in every scene, and in every moment. Is the actor believable as a self-absorbed broadcaster in the seventies, or an oil man dominating the American west in the 1880s, or a blind girl fleeing monsters in a forest? If so, we call it good acting.

Character is what an actor puts on to entertain us. But, everyone *has* character, too. It's what we're made of. The question is, what's our character like? Do we have good character, and if so, is it consistent?

Water baby.

The biblical book of Exodus tells of another baby who lived well over a thousand years before Jesus. The story picks up with the Israelite people enslaved in Egypt. As you can imagine, this wasn't a good situation for them. Held captive against their will, they suffered through life as Pharaoh's cheap labour force.

Pharaoh had a problem, however. The Israelites were gifted procreators. The swelling population concerned Egypt's leader (perhaps he feared an uprising) and so he ordered that all male children be slaughtered upon birth.

A certain Israelite priest and his wife were expecting, and the soon-to-be mother couldn't bear to see her newborn son skewered upon arrival. Unable to keep her secret (after managing to hide him for three months), she eventually placed him in a basket and sent him down the Nile. She must have thought this a better option than certain death for the boy. We're not told of the mother's intentions in the narrative, but apparently the child was dropped in near a royal bathing spot. Pharaoh's daughter spotted the basket, heard the crying baby, and eventually adopted him.

She named the boy Moses. One of the reasons she may have named him as she did was because "Moses" sounded like the Hebrew word for "draw out." This was fitting since she "drew him from the water."[79] Moses grew up as an Egyptian prince, and life looked good for him. One day, however, he got himself into trouble. He had a traumatic identity crisis and ended up murdering an Egyptian who was beating on a Hebrew slave. Moses buried the body in the sand, and hoped no one would notice. People noticed.

Fearing for his life, he fled Egypt, got married and became a shepherd. Moses thought he'd live out his days in relative anonymity. He was able to for about forty years, until one day a bush started speaking to him. The bush got his attention, obviously.[80]

Let's press pause and pick back up with Moses in a few pages. His story gets more interesting.

Why we shouldn't give up on God so easily.

In part two we empathized with Ricky Bobby who "likes baby Jesus the best." Baby Jesus is the version of Jesus he most naturally relates to. It's easy to see where Ricky Bobby's coming from. We might like baby Jesus better than the other perspectives of God found in the Bible, especially when we consider the whole book. Isn't the God of the Old Testament a tyrant? Who wants to get to know or serve a tyrannical God?

A struggle some people have in buying into and trusting the God of the Bible is rooted in doubt about his character. They've read, or heard, that he's mean and nasty in the Old Testament, but sweet and cuddly in the New Testament. This trips some of us up, so much so that we give up before doing any further exploration and toss the baby out with the bathwater.

Inconsistent character is a problem for us, especially when some people claim *"God is good."* The world was a harsh place back then, it still can be today. God's good character might seem incongruent with how much pain and suffering we see around us.[81] As my best friend's three-year-old exclaimed after tripping and hitting his head on a door frame the other day, "Why did God make hard things?!"

God's good character, however, is consistent throughout the entire biblical narrative. We simply may need some help in discovering it through various and specific biblical stories. Sometimes it can be hard to see the forest for the trees.

Learning how to read and understand the Bible is a process. It's a book of depth, genre variation, and was written by a host of authors over hundreds of years. We're taking a rather abbreviated look, but allow me to highlight some important approaches when reading the Bible in hopes of discovering God's consistent character within it.[82]

Do you see what I see?

Everyone looks at the world through a particular lens. This lens is shaped by our culture, upbringing, personality, and whether or not we were exposed to Justin Bieber at age thirteen or age thirty-five. Our age is a lens because it roots us in time. Culture changes over time. Your chances of liking Justin Bieber's music *may* (and I emphasize may to all those thirty-five-year-old Bieber fans) depend on how old you are. We view life through a lens shaped by our culture and the time we live in.

The people who wrote the Bible also had lenses, having also lived in particular times and cultures. This is true of the first biblical audience as well. Books of the Bible weren't written to sit on the shelf and collect dust. They are letters, poetic books, historical documents, biographies, sermons, laments, and even ancient forms of legislation. They were read aloud, memorized, sung and studied. They still are.

When we read the Bible we must consider the lens of the writer, the lens of the reader, the time it was written in, the culture it was written in, the events surrounding its writing, the genre it's written in, and many other factors. It's remarkable that the Bible still carries such immediate, profound and comforting truth for today's average reader considering its complexity and depth.

Simple and complex.

The Bible is complex in nature. Understanding this is part of reading it properly. Part of the beauty of the Bible, however, is that we can still read it and simply be inspired, encouraged, or morally challenged. Mark, for example, wrote this passage almost two millennia ago:

> And they were bringing children to him that he might touch them, and the disciples rebuked them. But when Jesus saw it, he was indignant and said to them, "Let the children come to me; do not hinder them, for to such belongs the kingdom of God. Truly, I say to you, whoever does not receive the kingdom of God like a child shall not enter it." And he took them in his arms and blessed them, laying his hands on them.[83]

This is a simple story. Parents wanted the miracle-man to bless their children, but Jesus' friends shooed them away. Jesus, on the other hand, didn't tell the kids off for getting his robes dirty. Instead, he put his friends in their place. *Kids matter! Can't you see that?* Then, Jesus took the kids in his arms and blessed them.

We won't spend time unpacking the ancient world's view of and treatment of children. We won't spend time getting into the dramatic theological importance this has on understanding Jesus' mission and message. Doing both these things, however, would give us profound insight into the importance of Jesus' actions that day. It's clear from his life that he believed kids were *whole* human beings with rights, and needs, and were deserving of love.[84] This passage, all on its lonesome, is simply moving, encouraging and humbling. It's a simple message, but it has a complex background.

The Bible has depth to be explored, but also speaks with simplicity, immediacy and conviction. It has lovely bits and nasty bits. The lovely bits of the Bible are just as complex as the nasty bits; we're just more comfortable with them, so we don't ask as many questions.

So, what do we do with the nasty and complex bits of the Bible, the ones we're not so comfortable with? What about the ones surrounding God's actions in the Old Testament? How do they line up with nice-guy Jesus? Do they line up at all?

What's God's first impression?

As we saw in part three, the first impression someone makes on us can be a lasting one. Journalists put the most important information at the top of the article. The opening scene of a play will set the tone of the production. We dress up for job interviews. First impressions matter. Our first impression of God in the Bible is important. It's also a good one.

The first thing we learn about God in the book of Genesis is that he's creative and generous. Some read Genesis 1 as an ancient poem, and some read it literally. Regardless of your interpretation, God comes across in a positive light.

In Genesis 1 God *makes* everything and *gives* everything life. He calls creation good, and blesses humanity with the task of stewarding it. He creates man and woman in his image, establishing the basis for our need of community, and places them in a garden. Enter God, stage right. He's looking pretty good for a mighty, cosmic superpower.

This is the stage the Bible sets, and how the author of Genesis introduces us to God. Interestingly, it's also how the Bible ends, with God *renewing* the world and blessing humanity. We read all about gardens, trees and rivers in Revelation too.

When asking if Jesus is different than the God of the Old Testament, are we considering our first impression of God in Genesis? When Jesus is renewing people's sight, calming the waves, and healing lepers, are we comparing these actions to Genesis 1 and 2? God *makes* the world in Genesis. Jesus brings *renewal* to it in the gospels.

Life and death. Lost and found.

The story starts out well in Genesis, but it goes south soon enough. Humans mistrust this creative, generous God, and rebel. They mistrust God, the life-giver, and begin to trust solely in themselves. When faced with a choice, they choose something other than the God who made them.

In the biblical narrative this means they've chosen death. When they step away from the giver-of-life, what are they stepping towards? This is why, as many have noted, the Bible's main message isn't about goodness or badness. It's about life and death. Jesus didn't come to turn bad people into good people but to bring dead people back to life, back to God. Through Jesus, God is giving us *back* the life we previously discarded.

In Genesis the world gets messy, fast, and humans end up learning the hard way. This means they end up lying to, stealing from, abusing and killing one another. The world can be a nasty place. God, however, endeavours throughout the biblical story to reconcile us back to himself, to bring us *back to life*. But time and again humans reject God, and end up getting themselves into more and more trouble. God kept reaching out. Humans kept running away.

In Luke's gospel Jesus tells two stories of loss and redemption.[85] In the first, a man loses one out of a hundred of his sheep. Jesus says he searches for it high and low, finds it, and returns home with great joy. In the second, a woman loses one out of ten coins, but values it so greatly she scours the house until it is found. In both stories, both characters invite their friends over to celebrate the recovery of what they obviously felt was so precious.

Jesus' final story in chapter 15 is about two brothers and their father. One of them rejects the father, demands an early inheritance, leaves home, squanders all the money, and ends up living with pigs. One day he remembers how much better he had it at home, so he decides to make his way back. Jesus tells us that when the father sees him coming "from a long way off" he got up, ran to his son, and embraced him. Guess what he did next? You guessed it. He throws a big party.

This story is an illustrated and simplified version of the entire biblical narrative.[86] Notice the physical action of the main characters in all three stories. In every circumstance (one out of a hundred sheep, one out of ten coins, and one out of two sons) all three characters move toward, or go in search of, what has been lost.

Jesus' stories tell us much about how he thinks God operates and what his character is like. It would seem Jesus thinks God is determined to recover what was lost, and desperate to hold it near again.

An old hymn, written by twenty-year-old Robert Robinson in 1757,[87] wrestles with this narrative from one man's perspective beautifully:

Jesus sought me when a stranger,
wandering from the fold of God;
he, to rescue me from danger,
interposed his precious blood.

O to grace how great a debtor
daily I'm constrained to be!

Let thy goodness, like a fetter,
bind my wandering heart to thee.
Prone to wander, Lord, I feel it,
prone to leave the God I love;
here's my heart, O take and seal it,
seal it for thy courts above.

What about all the nasty bits?

It's easy to read about bloody battles, animal sacrifices, and slave treatment laws, and then make unfair judgements on ancient cultures. First of all, we in the twenty-first century don't exactly have it all together ourselves. Our criticism should be tempered.

If we think we can divorce ourselves from the reality that the world is a nasty place, we're wrong. Even if you don't own slaves, you likely contribute to some form of slavery based on the items you purchase every week. This is a sobering thought, but it reminds us that our highly prized Western individualism is false. We're a human family, and are all connected.

Second, are we considering the time and culture the Bible was written in? How was the way the Israelites did things (under God's instruction) different than how other cultures did them? Few of us are experts in ancient Near Eastern culture, so perhaps we should admit our ignorance and investigate further.

Biblical laws about marriage, slavery, child rearing, farming, theft, murder and adultery are rooted in a time different from our own. We live thousands of years later, and are far more evolved—at least we're supposed to be.

The Israelite God was, like Jesus, morally and ethically progressive, just, and generous in many ways other culture's deities were not. There are many examples we could point to. We see in Genesis and Exodus, for example, that God invented weekends. People needed to take a break after working for six days. God commands this.

There are some stories wherein God instructs the Israelites to do things we might find horrendous today. These actions, we must remember, are rooted in a certain time and culture. Conflict, peace, and cultural and moral progression looked differently than it may look now.

Why is God angry?

I've seen parents get angry for no reason. I recently saw a caregiver act so impatiently (borderline abusive) that I nearly stepped in and did something about it. My heart began to race, and my palms began to sweat. You shouldn't treat children that way.

I've also seen parents get justifiably angry. Perhaps Jimmy hit Sally with a ruler in the face. No parent should stand for that. Sally needs to be protected, and Jimmy needs to be disciplined. Children need patience and lots of love. Disciplining a child is part of loving a child. Discipline must be carried out in correct measure and mode, however.

A child's growth and development depends on discipline. The Bible calls humans God's children, his creation. He wants what's best for us, and that kind of parenting takes time, energy, commitment and love. It takes an extra-long time when you give the beings you create free will, and commit to honouring it.

When considering God's anger and actions in the Old Testament, we should always ask *why* he is angry and *what* his response is in light of humanity's actions. If we are his creation (his children), how is he parenting us? What's the overall journey? An overwhelming sense of patience and love emerges from the Biblical picture of God when we consider his character over thousands and thousands of years.

Please hear me. I'm not saying that biblical hardships (from war, to hunger, to slavery) is God's way of teaching humanity a lesson. That's far too simplistic and ultimately the opposite of the biblical message. As we already established, the world is a broken place, and humans have free will. We must take responsibility for our actions, and the consequences of them. The Bible would teach that God is, however, in the middle of all this and working things out for the good. He's involved, he's in the thick of it.

From time to time in the Bible we see God bring correction and discipline, but any good parent would agree this is necessary for the growth of a child. Not to get ahead of ourselves, but as much as humanity could use a swift kick in the pants now and then, how does God ultimately react to our rebellion? What is his big solution to the problem? We see how ancient kings and emperors dealt with rebellion. Rebellions will be brutally crushed, said the Persians, Babylonians and Romans.

The biblical narrative tells us God ultimately fixes the world's problem of evil. He does so not by punishing it, but by absorbing evil through Jesus' sacrifice on the cross. Through Jesus, God inhaled death, and exhaled life. As one of my old professors used to say: grace is getting what you don't deserve, and mercy is not getting what you deserve. The Bible says that through Jesus, humanity receives both grace *and* mercy.[89]

Time is of the essence.

God spoke to and acted in ways that the people of that time understood. He functioned within culture. Some argue the best way to read the Bible is to look for the redemptive movement within each book or story.[90] Is God trying to move humanity forward on issues of morality, justice and peace? What is the direction in each story, and time? What's the direction in the broader biblical narrative? Paul sees it this way in a letter to a group of people called the Galatians:

> But when the fullness of time had come, God sent forth his Son, born of woman, born under the law, to redeem those who were under the law, so that we might receive adoption as sons. And because you are sons, God has sent the Spirit of his Son into our hearts, crying, "Abba! Father!" So you are no longer a slave, but a son, and if a son, then an heir through God.[91]

This phrase "fullness of time" is important. It means, amongst other things, "just the right time." It means the God of the Bible had a plan, and humanity was on a journey. Jesus came when the time was right. There were a lot of humans who lived before Jesus, more have lived since and still more are being born every day. The biblical story says we're all part of one giant journey.[92]

Growth takes time. As a young man I often get frustrated with how slow life seems to progress. When will *real* life kick in? When will I get *there*? Because I'm a Christian I believe God is deeply invested in my life. I often have to remind myself that God is usually more like a slow cooker than a microwave.

How long does it usually take for you to grow or progress? I'm certainly not a quick learner. Paul wrote this to a group of Christians living in Rome as he shared his struggle to learn and grow:

> I don't understand what I do. I don't do what I want to do. Instead, I do what I hate to do. I do what I don't want to do.[93]

Does Paul sound a little turned around? Have you ever felt this way? My journey will take time. Your journey will take time. Humanity's collective journey will take time.

Was Jesus always cuddly?

Jesus was warm, kind and servant-hearted, but he wasn't made of cotton candy. The Bible tells us Jesus got angry with self-righteous people, trashed the Temple in Jerusalem, and allowed himself to be tortured and killed for the good of humankind.[94] Jesus also began his life on the run from a mass murderer. Both the Old Testament and the New showcase how brutal life can be. Jesus wasn't as cuddly as some have made him out to be.

Jesus lived in the real world, faced real problems, and confronted real issues. As warm and inviting as he was, he wouldn't stand for hate or exploitation, either. Jesus got his hands dirty. He got angry because he cared about people, and cared about justice. He turned the other cheek, but when the occasion called for it (usually when people were being mistreated), he stood his ground.[95]

Recently, a movie about the biblical story of Noah's ark was released.[96] The writer/director emphasized a strong theme in the Noah story: the tension between justice and mercy. This is God's dilemma throughout the Bible. Justice matters—the wrong in the world needs to be dealt with. God acts, however, with great patience and mercy. God balances justice and mercy. This is no easy task.

In Jesus we see this tension resolved. The Bible teaches that Jesus loved us enough to die on a cross and therefore, we've received mercy. God takes death upon himself, on our behalf, and gifts us with life instead.[97]

What's the big picture?

Sometimes biblical stories can seem harsh or unreasonable. One reason
they might seem this way is because we choose to read them in a vacuum. This would be like watching the scene in *Home Alone* when Kevin's
mom sends him to bed without any dinner, and then neglecting to watch
the rest of the movie. We are in danger of missing the main point if we
overemphasize a singular scene.

We ignore the *whole* narrative when we pick out individual stories
and base entire world views, or God-views, on them. When we investigate the entire Bible, what's the big picture? Perhaps God's character
throughout is overwhelmingly generous and patient, considering how
unruly humankind has been throughout the ages.

Through all of the war, struggle, brokenness and pain, what's
the resounding call we hear from God? What's his overarching posture
toward the human race? What's the *main point*?

These are just a few considerations we should make while reading
the Bible, and especially the Old Testament. Back to Moses.

Water baby, part II.

We left Moses herding sheep and living in exile after fleeing Egypt. One
day he was tending to his flock when he came across a bush. The bush
was on fire, but wasn't disintegrating. Exodus tells us God spoke to Moses
through the bush and told him to go back to Egypt to lead his people out
of bondage.

A friend of mine recently made me aware of something in this
story I hadn't yet considered. He noted that God chose to speak *through
a bush*. A bush, not a giant tree or a mighty thunderstorm. A bush doesn't
seem too impressive, does it? He thought it telling that the Israelite's
entire narrative depended on Moses saying, *Hmm, what's that over there?
Think I'll check it out.* In the words of Mr. Dryden, in *Lawrence of Arabia*:
"Big things have small beginnings."[99]

God says go. Go and lead the people in a divinely ordained libera-
tion. Moses protests. He does so for a number of reasons. First, he's an
exiled murderer. Moses may be worried he isn't likely to receive a warm
welcome back in Egypt. Second, he's concerned the Israelites won't
follow him as their leader. Third, he's not convinced simply ordering

Pharaoh to release the slaves will mean Pharaoh will do so. These three excuses are understandable, but God persists. Moses is the man for the job, and God will help him. Finally, Moses gets desperate and tells God he's simply not good at public speaking.[100] That didn't fly either. Moses ends up going back to Egypt.

You may have heard the rest of the story. God gives little old Moses the ability to lead the people, perform miracles, and even part a giant body of water. God ultimately delivers the Israelites from Egypt, an unexpected Exodus.[101]

Always near.

Moses didn't look impressive, and maybe that's the point. God works *through* him. Moses' life is dramatic and famous. His origins are humble, however. So is what he seemed to bring to the table as a leader. The key was that God was *with* him.

A man named Abraham lived hundreds of years before Moses. God promised him he'd be the father of a great nation. The problem was that Abraham and his wife were pushing one hundred years old when God promised this. Even so, they miraculously had a son. The key, again, was that God was *with* them. He was also *with* their son when he grew up.[102]

David was a shepherd boy. When an army led by a man who stood over eight feet tall threatened the Israelites, David volunteered to kill him.[103] Because David was just a kid, and not even enrolled in the military, people laughed at the idea. David's conversation with his king (named Saul) reveals to us his confidence despite his position, experience or size.

> "The LORD saved me from the paw of the lion. He saved me from the paw of the bear. And he'll save me from the powerful hand of this Philistine too."
>
> Saul said to David, "Go. And may the LORD be with you."[104]

David strutted out onto the battlefield with little more than a slingshot, and the rest is history. He became *David the giant slayer.*

In part three we looked at the story of an angelic invitation to the shepherds to visit the newborn baby Jesus. The shepherd's presence at the manger actually has some layers: David once wrote a poem about how God is like a shepherd. People still memorize it today:

> The Lord is my shepherd; I shall not want.
> He makes me lie down in green pastures. He leads me beside still waters.
> He restores my soul. He leads me in paths of righteousness for his name's sake.
> Even though I walk through the valley of the shadow of death, I will fear no evil, for you are with me; your rod and your staff, they comfort me.
> You prepare a table before me in the presence of my enemies; You anoint my head with oil; my cup overflows.
> Surely goodness and mercy shall follow me all the days of my life, and I shall dwell in the house of the Lord forever.[105]

David lived about a thousand years before Jesus and hailed from the same town Jesus did: Bethlehem.

The poem shows us that David had a fairly personal, intimate view of God. David sees God in a good, even humble, light. Good shepherds reminded David of his good God. David felt that God was very much *with* him.

Just as in the Christmas narrative, story after story in the Bible's Old Testament embodies the balance of the spectacular coupled with the unspectacular. The unimpressive infused with the impressive. The big and the small. The powerful and the meek.

As we saw in part three, Luke's gospel tells us Mary was instructed to name her son *Immanuel*, meaning *God with us*. In Jesus we meet a familiar face. A God who defines himself by his love toward us. His desire to be near and his passion to help us are unavoidable themes throughout the entire biblical narrative.

Considering God's action through the lives of many ordinary Old Testament personalities like Moses, Abraham, Joseph, Hannah, David, Jonah, Rahab, Gideon, Elijah, and many more, why are we surprised when we meet Mary and Joseph, the shepherds and the wise men?

Perhaps we shouldn't be surprised to discover the perfect balance of humility and power in the baby lying in the manger. This God has been *with* us before. Now he's *with* us in the person of Jesus. God's story is consistent, and he never breaks character.

Part Six
Grasping Greatness

Come in and know me better, man!
-The Ghost of Christmas Present, *A Christmas Carol*

King who?

A friend of mine got married last year. Part gift and part excuse for a father-son trip, his dad took him on an excursion many people only dream of. A month or so before the wedding they hopped on a plane and flew to Uganda. My friend's been to Africa on several occasions, but this time was different. This time, they joined up with a jungle expedition and set off in search of mountain gorillas.

The tour group spent two days hiking through dense jungle, tracking the giant apes in hopes of catching a glimpse. After hours of hiking and sweating through the wilderness, their guide finally noticed marks of gorilla life. Bent grass, droppings, and other signs meant King Kong wasn't far off.

The guide told my friend to be quiet and stay low. They crouched slowly toward what seemed like nothing. Then, rising from the grass, several black, hairy rounded shapes came into view. They'd found the band they were searching for.

The nearest creature was a three-hundred-pound silverback. They snuck closer and closer. The guide knew how close they were able to get without disturbing the animals. Edging nearer, he bent a blade of grass over so the tourists could get a better look. It was one blade too many.

The silverback slowly lifted his head and shifted his eyes toward the group. He obviously knew he was being watched, and was alright with it, until they came a little too close. In the blink of an eye he was up on all-fours, and bolted toward the group. He covered a few feet in terrifying speed. My friend didn't react. He didn't scream or run. He just stood still.

He remained motionless, not because the guide trained him to freeze in the event of a charge, or because he was paralyzed by fear. In his words: "I didn't have time to move. He was three feet away before I even had time to react. I knew they were quick, but I had no idea *how* quick until I saw them first hand."

Fortunately Kong stopped in his tracks after a few feet. He didn't intend to hurt anyone, just show the tourists who was boss and instill a little respect. My friend was thankful, and didn't think marriage was so scary after his experience in Uganda.

Lots of people I've talked to relate to God like they might a silverback gorilla. They may be curious, and perhaps even show a little respect. Ultimately, however, they experience fear or trepidation when thinking about the divine. You may know someone who makes jokes like, "Oh, I can't go to church. I'd burst into flames as soon as I walked through the door!" This says a lot about who they think God is, and how they think he operates.

After all, if God's so powerful, why would he want to have anything to do with us? Aren't we bothering him with our petty problems? Is he waiting for us to bend one more blade of grass before he bolts, threatening to tear us limb from limb? Is he perched up in heaven, just waiting for the chance to cause us to spontaneously combust? Is God cruel, impatient or dangerous?

Being a pastor I listen to people share about their spiritual perspectives or religious background all the time. Many share less-than-flattering views of God. Some of them grew up going to church, lived in "Christian" homes, and even lead others in church settings. Their primary understanding of God's nature, however, has been corrupted.

Guesswork.

Many people had great parents or caregivers, but just as many didn't. When a young man tells me he feels like God is always upset with him, or mustn't be interested in his daily goings on (and this is a common theme), I usually ask him a few questions. One of the first: *What was life at home like growing up?*

I'm no psychiatrist, but many pastors will tell you there tends to be a common thread that runs between people's vision of God and their experience of childhood. Authority figures leave an impression on us when we're young. If dad or mom is cruel, impatient, uninterested, or perhaps not even present, we can tend to project these traits onto others later in life. Maybe we even project them onto God.

This isn't to say people who have had nasty childhoods can never grasp the notion of a loving God—quite the opposite. Many have had their paradigm of God turned upside down and inside out after learning about and getting to know the love of God through the story and person of Jesus.

I have a friend who was abused by her father for years. This obviously caused her great pain, and so later in life she coped with lots of sex, drugs, alcohol and an eating disorder. One day she cracked. She and her husband had to seek help. She met with a Christian counsellor for a number of months. She learned about the true nature of the God of the Bible, and began to sense the pain subsiding. She started to heal, and eventually even began the process of forgiving her father. She also chose to trust God in deeper ways.

Today, she's one of the brightest, warmest people I know—a loving wife, mother and businesswoman. She's proudly shared her story with hundreds of people (which is not an easy thing to do); a testament to the possibility of healing and hope.

My friend had a bad father, but her experience of Jesus transformed her pain into joy and her emptiness into fulfilment. She'll tell you this was primarily because she learned who Jesus was, and chose to trust him.

Some of us have had bad parents, but even the best parents in the world aren't perfect. The Bible teaches that God is perfect, however. Parents, friends, spouses or children have the potential to mirror his character, but they also have the potential to distort it.

No one is totally like God, not even the sweetest, kindest, sweater-knitting, cookie-baking grandmother you know. Grandma's not perfect. No one is. This is why the Bible says God chose to live among us in the person of Jesus. The first Christians believed that God wanted us to truly know who he was and did this through Jesus' arrival. He wanted to make himself clear. Someone once put it this way, by paraphrasing a portion of John's gospel:

> The Word became flesh and blood, and moved into the neighbourhood. We saw him with our own eyes,
> the one-of-a-kind glory, like Father, like Son, Generous inside and out, true from start to finish.[106]

If fear and trepidation holds us back from being open to God, maybe we're missing the point of Christmas altogether. Perhaps we're speculating about God's nature, when we should be looking at Jesus instead. Another friend of mine says it like this: if you want to know what God's like, don't guess!

Cut from the same cloth.

My dad and I are quite similar. We relate well to one another because we share a number of traits. We also look a lot alike. As I age, I notice more and more of my dad's personality in mine. In my case, this isn't a bad thing—he's a great guy. Remember what the book of Hebrews said about Jesus and God?

> He is the radiance of the glory of God and the exact imprint of his nature, and he upholds the universe by the word of his power.[107]

And also Paul in Colossians:

> He is the image of the invisible God...[108]

And:

> For in him the whole fullness of deity dwells bodily...[109]

The Bible teaches we can know what God is like by looking at Jesus. Many believe this is why he's the most important figure in history, and why his influence and fame can't be stamped out.

Christians have sometimes horribly misrepresented Jesus over the years, yet his reputation for love and compassion stands strong. How good a person do you have to be to have endured centuries of intentional and unintentional distortion? Despite the bad rap many have given Christianity, Jesus' reputation endures.

The night before he died, Jesus assembled his closest friends and followers. He shared a meal with them and downloaded everything he wanted them to remember. It appears that he knew he was going to die, and so his final moments with his disciples are words to note in John's gospel.[110]

Around the dinner table one of his friends, Philip, was struggling with what many of us wrestle with today. As we saw in part one, many people like Jesus, but we have a hard time accepting his divinity. Philip was in the same boat. The gospels say Jesus healed blind people, fed thousands by miraculously multiplying a few pieces of bread and some fish, cast demons out of strong and violent men, and even raised at least one person from the dead. In spite of all this, Philip still struggled to believe that Jesus *was actually* God amongst them.

Sometimes people say they might believe in God if he gave them some sort of clear sign of his existence. This didn't seem to work for Philip, even when the sign was staring him in the face, controlling the weather, and walking on water. During supper, while Jesus was sharing his final lesson, Philip piped up:

> Philip said to him, "Lord, show us the Father, and it is enough for us." Jesus said to him, "Have I been with you so long, and you still do not know me, Philip? Whoever has seen me has seen the Father. How can you say, 'Show us the Father'? Do you not believe that I am in the Father and the Father is in me? The words that I say to you I do not speak on my own authority, but the Father who dwells in me does his works. Believe me that I am in the Father and the Father is in me, or else believe on account of the works themselves.[111]

For those who try to use the gospels to argue that Jesus never claimed to be God, this is a challenging passage. Who's the "Father" Jesus speaks of? The common consensus is that he's referring to the Israelites' one-true God.

To say that this is a bold statement from Jesus would be a massive understatement. According to him, the man sitting at the table sharing a meal with them and the God who created the universe were one and the same.

Jesus says, *My Dad and I are cut from the same cloth. I carry his character. If you want to know what the one-true God of the universe is like, watch me...Oh, and pass the bread sticks.*

Closed fridges can't wash feet.

A while back I had a couple of friends over and hadn't prepared to host them. I realized I should probably try to be a good friend and offer them *something*. I pulled a bag of cookies from the cupboard and opened the fridge to grab the milk. Lifting the carton, I discovered there was little milk left in it. In a moment I'll regret for the rest of my life I told them I had cookies, but not enough milk to go around *and* enough for me to use the next day. I could only offer them water. I didn't think that moment through.

Being good (and quick-witted) friends they immediately exposed my selfish sense of self-preservation, and proceeded to mock me for it. I realized it too, and tried to backpedal. *Of course they were welcome to the milk.* Awkward.

Now whenever they're over and I offer them tea, or juice, or water, or anything, they respond with, "Except milk, right?" We laugh, and it's a good reminder of how much I have to learn about hospitality and generosity. I still can't believe I did that.

Jesus was a better host than me. The night before he was crucified, John says Jesus did something ridiculous, right in the middle of dinner. The next scene might sound bizarre because Jesus' actions are rooted in an ancient culture. Believe me when I tell you that his actions were even more confounding back then.

> Jesus, knowing that the Father had given all things into his hands, and that he had come from God and was going back to God, rose from supper. He laid aside his outer garments, and taking a towel, tied it around his waist. Then he poured water into a basin and began to wash the disciples' feet and to wipe them with the towel that was wrapped around him.[112]

During dinner parties in Jewish homes it was customary to wash your guest's feet. People wore sandals all the time back then, and living in the dusty Near East meant daily dealings with dirty feet. When guests sat on the floor and reclined for supper (as you still do in some of the Near East today) it was nice to have clean feet.

The host of the party didn't *personally* wash everyone's feet, of course. Servants did this, specifically the lowest, most unimportant servant in the household. I've heard some suggest this job was so degrading and undignified that first century Jewish masters would *never* force Jewish servants to wash feet—non-Jewish servants would be left to do that kind of dirty work.[113]

John's account of the foot washing is strategic. It's a key moment in the meal, and the gospel story in general. It's probably one of the reasons Philip asks to "see the Father," later on. Obviously Almighty God must be above this kind of work, and wouldn't stoop to wash feet. Jesus did.

This was mind-blowing for his friends: "Why would Jesus want to expose himself to my athlete's foot?" They must have thought. "I thought he was important! Important people don't wash feet!"

When Jesus came to Peter and tried to remove his Birkenstocks, Peter flipped his lid and outright rebuked his rabbi. Jesus responded by saying, *Pete, if you don't let me do this then you'll miss the whole point. This is what I'm all about, and if this doesn't happen then you can't be on the team.* Peter's reaction was: *Well then, toss me in at the deep end. Not just my feet, but all of me.* Peter signs up, still trying to work out what he was signing up for.[114]

John continues:

> When he had washed their feet and put on his outer garments and resumed his place, he said to them, "Do you understand what I have done to you? You call me Teacher and Lord, and you are right, for so I am. If I then, your Lord and Teacher, have washed your feet, you also ought to wash one another's feet. For I have given you an example, that you also should do just as I have done to you. Truly, truly, I say to you, a servant is not greater than his master, nor is a messenger greater than the one who sent him.[115]

How's that for an object lesson?

This vision of Jesus is important, and we see it all over the gospels. This is why people who claim to follow Jesus should be humble, kind, thoughtful, servant-hearted individuals. If you know a Christian who isn't like this, maybe you could offer to help them learn more about their faith by kindly asking if they'd like to wash your feet...or offer you the last drops of milk from their fridge.

How to be great (and look foolish doing it).

To say that Jesus rolled up his sleeves and got his hands dirty is too meagre a metaphor in describing his attitude while living alongside us. Jesus didn't just help humanity move house or unclog a drain. God amongst us, acting as Jesus did, goes beyond any comparable simile.

The foot-washing is a standout example of how low Jesus stooped. He became as humble as humanly possible in his culture. He wholeheartedly exemplified the words we hear from him in Matthew's gospel:

> You know that the rulers of the Gentiles lord it over them, and their great ones exercise authority over them. It shall not be so among you. But whoever would be great among you must be your servant and whoever would be first among you must be your slave, even as the Son of Man came not to be served but to serve, and to give his life as a ransom for many.[116]

Jesus correctly identifies how the world works. Your boss is top dog, and can make your life hell if she's in a bad mood. The older kids at school are tough, and can push you around if they want to. Silverbacks will always display control over their territory, usually with aggression and force.

This wasn't how Jesus did things. He made this even clearer a few short hours later when he allowed himself to be arrested, tortured, and crucified. He did this, he said, to serve humanity.

This drastically changed the course of history. As we noted in chapter one, humility as we know it today was only embraced in the West as virtue, post-Jesus. One historian speaks of people's choice of what to do with Jesus once they came to grips with his life and death:

Logically, they had just two options. Either Jesus was not as great as they had first thought, his crucifixion being evidence of his insignificance, or the notion of "greatness" itself had to be redefined to fit with the fact of his seemingly shameful end.[117]

The foot-washing was the precursor to the cross. The cross shows us, almost unfathomably, how much Jesus humbled himself. This act, the Bible teaches, was for the good of the world.

The manger, the foot washing and the cross affirm a foundational Christian truth: Jesus got filthy so we can be clean. Jesus is *the* example for Christian living. Following Jesus means living like he did—it means living humbly.

How low can you go?

I recently met a man who helps out at the local homeless shelter. Norman is in his fifties, has long hair, a beard, and a warm, unique face. Norman also has some physical challenges, including scoliosis. He wasn't diagnosed until he was a teenager, so everything seemed normal in his younger years. Things changed when he got to high school, however.

Norman was shorter than his high school classmates, and got teased for it. His back was bent, and this significantly affected the rest of his body in form and function. He had some rough years, and at one point ended up on the street. During this time, a former employer told him about Jesus, and Norman became a Christian.

Norman now has a steady job, a home, a truck, and serves at the shelter every week. I asked him what he does with his spare time. He told me he picks up things people don't want and delivers them to local charities. Norman collects goods and gives them to agencies in need, or sells them and donates the cash. He also likes to tell people he meets about Jesus. He agreed with me that serving at the shelter was a great way of sharing Jesus and his message. As Norman said, "It's about serving."

Norman seems to understand the Jesus we read about in the gospels. From this perspective, Norman is *great*. You don't have to look or sound impressive by other people's standards to make a difference. Jesus acted more like Norman than he did a three-hundred-pound silverback gorilla. Perhaps Norman has read these words from Paul in his letter to the Philippians:

> Do nothing from selfish ambition or conceit, but in humility count others more significant than yourselves. Let each of you look not only to his own interests, but also to the interests of others. Have this mind among yourselves, which is yours in Christ Jesus, who, though he was in the form of God, did not count equality with God a thing to be grasped, but emptied himself, by taking the form of a servant, being born in the likeness of men. And being found in human form, he humbled himself by becoming obedient to the point of death, even death on a cross. Therefore God has highly exalted him and bestowed on him the name that is above every name, so that at the name of Jesus every knee should bow, in heaven and on earth and under the earth, and every tongue confess that Jesus Christ is Lord, to the glory of God the Father.[118]

Before Jesus washed feet, blessed children, stood up for women's rights, healed sick people or died on a cross, he was content to be born quietly amongst us. His birth and infancy displayed how much God was willing to serve humanity. Jesus' greatness evidenced itself through his humility. Maybe that's what real greatness is in the first place.

An unlikely Christmas convert.

The passage from Philippians in the previous section has an introduction I left out. Paul begins it this way:

> ...make my joy complete by being of the same mind, maintaining the same love, united in spirit, intent on one purpose...[119]

Love, joy and togetherness would seem to be what many say Christmas is all about.

Other than what I find in the Bible, one of my all-time favourite stories is *A Christmas Carol* by Charles Dickens. I love the book, as well as a number of the film adaptations. The story of a nasty old curmudgeon's conversion to Christmas moves me every time.

Early on, Dickens introduces us to his story's main character: Ebenezer Scrooge. He's a distant, unfeeling, stingy old jerk. He also *hates* Christmas:

> Oh! But he was a tight fisted hand at the grindstone, Scrooge! A squeezing, wrenching, grasping, scraping, covetous old sinner. Hard and sharp a flint, from which no steel had ever struck out generous fire; secret, and self contained, and solitary as an oyster. The cold within me froze his old features, nipped his pointed nose, shrivelled his cheek, stiffened his gait; made his eyes red, his thin lips blue; and spoke out shrewdly in his grating voice. A frosty rime was on his head, and on his eyebrows, and his wiry chin. He carried his own low temperature always about with him; he iced his coffee in the dog-days; and didn't thaw in one degree at Christmas.[120]

When we first meet Scrooge he's cruel, cold, cranky, and closed off. He's also rich, but acts like he's poor, hoarding every penny, unwilling to share with anyone save the taxman. He doesn't have time for people, shows no mercy to his debtors, is feared by the entire city of London, and wants to be left alone.

You probably know at least some of the rest of the story. One night he's visited by a number of ghosts who open his eyes to the true meaning of the Christmas season. He realizes the horrible plight of the poor he's been ignoring, is thawed by the love of family and friends, and reflects on his troubled past. He also faces a cold, hard reality: life is short, and everybody dies one day. This one night brings about a dramatic conversion in Scrooge and sets him on a new course of good-hearted, benevolent living. One of Dickens' final descriptions of Scrooge is this:

> He became as good a friend, as good a master, and as good a man, as the good old city knew, or any other good old city, town, borough, in the good old world. Some people laughed to see the alteration in him, but he let them laugh, and little heeded them; for he was wise enough to know that nothing ever happened on this globe, for good, at which some people did not have their fill

of laughter in the outset...His own heart laughed and that was quite enough for him.[120]

Scrooge was no longer paralyzed by pride. His prior way of life saw only money compound, but his new way of life saw joy compound. His transformation didn't change his position in life. He still had money, and he still had power. What he did with his money and power changed, however. Instead of living in fear and only looking out for himself, he chose to live in love. He opened his heart to his family and neighbours, helped the needy, and lived generously. In short, Scrooge became humble. One writer defines humility this way:

> ...The noble choice to forgo your status, deploy your resources or use your influence for the good of others before yourself. More simply, you could say a humble person is marked by a willingness to hold power in service of others.[121]

Greatness, humility, love, joy, togetherness—perhaps they're all connected. Perhaps they have a root, an origin. I believe the baby in the manger, (later the foot-washing rabbi and the man on the cross) is our best example of that origin. Maybe grasping greatness begins with cradling the infant.

Part Seven
Making Room

Well, time passed slowly. Rudolf existed as best he could...during all that time, a strange and wonderful thing happened: Rudolf was growing up....And pretty soon he knew where he had to go: home.

-*Rudolf, The Red-Nosed Reindeer*

Breathing underwater.

A couple of years ago I visited a friend who lives in Hawaii. He offered me a bed and to tour me around the Big Island. Born and raised in paradise, Chris was the ideal guide. I had no idea how much I needed this kind of vacation. Sometimes I can be boring. Chris' way of life was anything but.

We hiked through the jungle, and swam in a remote waterfall. We dipped in natural hot springs nestled up to the ocean, and jumped off cliffs into the deep blue pacific. One cliff earned the nickname "the end of the world". Another was located at the southernmost tip of the United States. We stood on a 40-foot outcrop, looked into the vast horizon, and tried to spot Antarctica. He jumped. My mouth dried up. I eventually followed.

One morning Chris informed me we were heading to a unique spot. He told me to pack for a desert hike, but also be ready to swim. We drove into the middle of nowhere, an area covered in volcanic rock, parked the car on a dirt road, and pulled on our packs. As we trudged through the barren landscape, the snorkel and fins we carried felt a like a silly choice of hiking equipment. We wandered for a while, and then finally found what he was looking for. "Here it is." said Chris. "It's a lava tube!"

I had no idea what to expect as we descended into the dusty hole. The light soon disappeared, and a couple of headlamps lit our path. Not only were we deep underground, but we were in the middle of the desert. I've never felt more isolated in my life. If something went wrong here, we were on our own.

After about half an hour we reached what I thought was the end of the tube. I was wrong. Before us was a glassy pool, perfectly calm. We shone our headlamps on it. For a moment I thought I was looking at a perfect reflection of the cave's ceiling. I then realized what I saw was not the ceiling, but the bottom of the water source. The pool had perfect visibility. The rock formations were spectacular.

We got into our masks and fins, and into the water. It's eerie to swim in the pitch black. No stars, no moon, just a headlamp. Turn that off and you're blind as a bat. I bobbed up and down on the surface, occasionally diving to the bottom to have a look. Admittedly, it wasn't my bravest of days. Every crevice and hole I shone my lamp into looked like it might house an underwater movie monster. Chris was far braver. He jumped right in (after complaining about the cold water—Hawaiians hate cold water) and immediately began exploring the submerged caves. He swam between pillars, under big boulders, and squeezed into spots I refused to follow him through.

Later, we sat in the dark on a big rock and he told me about the times he'd been there before. Chris and his friends would hike a dive tank into the tube, share a regulator, and see how far the smaller tubes stretched from the main one. I thought this was reckless and foolish. I told him that. He's used to me saying things like this about his choice of recreational activities.

Chris didn't find this stuff reckless. He'd grown up on a boat and been on hundreds of unique dives. He knew what he was doing, trusted his equipment, and relied on his training. All these factors allowed Chris to experience and explore worlds I'd only dreamt of. Now, he was helping me experience them too.

One day Chris taught me how to scuba dive. We began in the hotel pool, and I learned about all the equipment. By the end of the training I was able to identify and utilize each part of the gear by myself. I was also able to submerge to the bottom of the pool and breathe underwater, something I *shouldn't* be able to do. Everyone knows humans can't breathe underwater.

Eventually we got into the ocean, and I had the time of my life. Thirty feet or so below the surface was another world, a place I'd only ever seen on screen. I consider myself relatively well travelled, but this was different. Most of the earth isn't covered by land, but by water. With a wetsuit and a tank I'd joined the ranks of humans who explore the most mysterious and bountiful environment on our planet. A small part of it, at least. The coral, the fish, the seaweed, and the spiky, nasty, dangerous looking things were in vibrant, high-definition. I kept thinking to myself, "This is real! Take in as much as you can!" It felt like a dream, but I couldn't pinch myself through the wetsuit to see if I'd snap out of it.

Sadly, many people will never scuba dive. Some aren't able to enjoy the sport because of health reasons, extreme phobias, inaccessibility, or cost. Many others, however, will never try it simply by choice. They decline the opportunity because it challenges a primal, hard-wired reality: *everyone knows humans can't breathe underwater.*

This keeps many from ever attempting a dive. We won't try it simply because it's too strange, too new, and takes us beyond our comfort zone. We aren't willing to trust the equipment or training. We won't listen to others who've experienced it before and exclaim, "It's totally worth it!"

Because of this, we'll never see the coral, the fish, the seaweed and the spiky, nasty, dangerous looking things the way divers do. We'll never stand on the bottom of the ocean, surrounded by sea life, and watch the sun shimmer and stream through forty feet of water, creating colours no screen saver can match. We'll miss out on experiencing a unique perspective of an environment that covers two-thirds of our planet. Can you really say you've seen the world if you've never been to the bottom of the ocean and stayed there a while?

Scuba diving forces us to let go of preconceived assumptions, and even some fear. We reject a reality we know to be true (humans can't breathe underwater), and learn to trust the training we receive and the equipment we're using. We learn a new manner of breathing. When we do all this, we get to experience the world in a way we never have before.

Some of us have grown up *knowing* a few things. Things like: power and humility don't mix; God is distant and unfeeling; love must be earned. I believe the baby in the manger challenges these assumptions.

Dr. J.

Trusting and following Jesus is like choosing to scuba dive. We relinquish some thinking we *know* to be true, and dive into the unknown. We trust our new breath and embrace new truths we've recently discovered. We dive in with faith, and the world never looks the same again.

But, you might ask, isn't faith about being totally sure about what you're placing your faith *in*? Well, here's a question in response. Is faith about assurance, or is faith about trust?

Maybe it's a little of both.

What if we've got questions? What if we're screwed up? What if we feel we're not cut out for this kind of trust and risk?

Well, me too.

I've got questions, I'm screwed up, and I constantly wonder if I'm cut out for this kind of life. Every Christian I know feels the same way. Curiosity simply gave way to exploration, and exploration gave way to trust. The Christian life is about learning to trust more every day.

Luke's gospel holds a story about a short man named Zacchaeus.[122] Zacch was a tax collector in a place called Jericho. Tax collectors weren't popular in Jesus' day, as you might imagine. They were known for extortion and fraud. Luke tells us Zacch was the *chief* tax collector in Jericho. He was unpopular and rich.

One day Jesus came to Jericho. Zacch had heard about him and wanted a closer look. Because Jesus was so popular, and Zacch was so short, the crowds around him made it impossible for Zacch to catch a glimpse. Eventually he climbed a tree to try and spot Jesus.

The story goes that Jesus noticed him, told him to climb down, and invited himself over for dinner. This might seem like rude behaviour, but it would have been a great honour for Zacch to host a popular rabbi like Jesus. A bunch of people weren't happy about Jesus' dinner plans, however. They must have thought: *Why is he eating with this guy? This guy's a crook!* Because of his line of work Zacchaeus was hated and marginalized by almost everyone.

Jesus noticed Zacch's curiosity, and opened his hand in friendship to him. Zacch was overjoyed. Read more of the story in Luke 19, if you like.

Mark tells us that Jesus once said:

> Those who are well have no need of a physician, but those who are sick. I came not to call the righteous, but sinners.[123]

We might not like the word "sinner," but all it really means is that someone isn't perfect. It doesn't mean someone isn't worthy of love or wasn't created with a purpose. Regardless of who we think Jesus is, or how many church services we may or may not have attended, no one's got it *all* together. By this definition, everyone's in the same boat. Knowing we've got problems isn't the end of the world. It's actually essential in understanding Jesus and the gospel.

Way back in part two we learned that "gospel" means good news. The good news is that Jesus came to heal the sick, and invite the sinners back home into his family. God isn't surprised by our condition, or unwilling to help us out of it. He's full of compassion and wants to help. He'd love to share a meal with us, just like he did with Zacchaeus.

Think about all the miracles Jesus performed: making blind people see, deaf people hear, lame people walk, curing lepers of their disease. What if all those miracles had a deeper meaning? What if they were physical metaphors for our human condition? What if Jesus was more than just a nice guy, but a living, breathing, walking example of God's invitation to wholeness and fulfillment?

A lot of people who are a part of my church today didn't grow up in one. Many of them investigated Jesus and the gospel, and chose to follow him later in life. A number of them share the same story when they talk about their journey toward the Christian faith. It usually sounds something like this:

> *I felt like something was missing, and I couldn't put my finger on it. I tried everything, but nothing brought the kind of fulfillment and purpose I was looking for. I sensed life was about more than money, my job, pleasure, morality, even friends and family. As good as all those things are, they didn't fully satisfy me. I was looking for something deeper, something more.*

*Upon my discovery of Jesus and the gospel, I found what I realized
I had been searching for my entire life. Sure, life can still be hard,
and I'm certainly not perfect, but I've experienced love, fulfilment
and purpose like I never did before I started following Jesus.*

Even though I grew up going to church, I felt similar to my friends at
different points throughout my life. I know I'm not perfect either, and
life will always have its ups and downs, but I'm daily choosing to accept
Jesus' invitation into life the way he designed it to be—life *with* him.

Solid as a sponge.

Peter was one of Jesus' first disciples. He was great, I love that guy. I don't
mean I love him because he was inspiring or noteworthy when it came to
the strength of his faith. I just find him entertaining. He's like that friend
who's always saying and doing stupid stuff, and making you shake your
head: *Oh Pete, I love that guy.*

To me, Peter's one of the funniest characters in the Bible. He's
funny because Jesus nicknamed him "the rock." Ironically, however, Peter
was about as solid as a sponge. He had a couple shining moments, but
much of what we see about him in the gospels concern his losses, not his
wins. The theme of contrast continues.

One day Jesus asked Peter who he thought Jesus was. Peter knocks
it out of the park: *You're God!* he exclaimed. In the next story Jesus pre-
dicts his death. Peter didn't like the sound of this one bit, so he jumped
in: *No way that's happening! Quit talking like that!* Peter didn't have a
problem identifying Jesus as God. He also didn't mind putting God in his
place once in a while.[124] Cheeky Pete.

In part six we looked at a dinner wherein Jesus washed his friends'
feet. At that dinner Peter actually told Jesus he'd never leave him, and
that he'd even die for him.[125]

When Jesus got up from the table and began preparing to wash his
friends' feet, the room must have been hushed. When he walked toward
Peter and tried to wash his feet, Peter exclaimed, *No way!* You might remember that in the next breath he jumped in at the deep end, signing on
for life, all without fully understanding what he'd signed on for.[126]

Later that night, Jesus was praying in a garden and asked his friends to join him. John tells us Jesus was in agony, or severe distress, aware that his crucifixion was just hours away. The disciples kept falling asleep, including Peter.[127]

When a mob came to arrest Jesus, Peter sprang into action and sliced the ear off of someone trying to cuff his rabbi. Jesus told Peter to put his sword away, and healed the man. Nice save, Jesus.[128] Peter then bolted, along with the rest of the disciples, abandoning Jesus to his arrestors.[129]

Later that night, during Jesus' trial, Peter snuck into the courthouse courtyard to see what was happening. Several people noticed him and said, *Hey, I know you! You're with Jesus, aren't you?* Peter flat out denied it three times, and cursed Jesus. Then he ran off again in shame, bawling his eyes out.[130] Let's recap. Within the span of about six hours, Peter has:

Told Jesus off for trying to wash his feet.
Changed his mind and opted for the dunk tank.
Fallen asleep when Jesus was having the worst night of his life.
Swashbuckled the ear off a guy (in defence of a rabbi defined by a non-violent life ethic).
Run off into the bushes like a scaredy-pants.
Snuck into the back of a courthouse to spy on Jesus' trial.
Totally thrown Jesus under the bus by lying, saying he and Jesus had no association.
Cursed Jesus.
Run off again, and cried in a corner.

Question: Do you think Jesus chose Peter because of how stable, unflinching and sure he was of what being a follower of his meant? Another question: Do you think Jesus needs us to be perfectly stable, unflinching and totally sure of what we'd be getting into if we started to trust and follow him?

Peter was compelled by, and drawn to Jesus. He was just like the shepherds and wise men. They couldn't shake him. They didn't know all the answers, *but they couldn't shake Jesus.* They'd never heard of, or met anyone like him.

Once, John tells us, a large group of people quit Jesus' fan club when he said some difficult stuff for them to hear.[131] In essence, Jesus was claiming to be God. When loads of people took off after hearing such challenging words, he asked his closest friends if they wanted to leave him, too. Peter piped up on behalf of the group:

> Lord, to whom shall we go? You have the words of eternal life, and we have believed, and have come to know, that you are the Holy One of God.[132]

Peter, I love that guy.

Not going anywhere.

You'll be happy to hear that Peter's journey got better. He learned to trust Jesus more and more every day. He still made mistakes, but he got less spongy and more rock-like as the years rolled on. He grew because he relied on Jesus. What's interesting is that Peter only hung out with Jesus for a maximum of three years.

After Jesus' death, the Bible tells us that Jesus rose from the dead.[133] As we noted earlier, the Bible teaches that Jesus inhaled death and exhaled life. The first Christians believed we can truly *live* because Jesus lives. The Bible then says that Jesus physically left the earth.[134] This would have been a massive let down for his friends if Jesus hadn't prepared them for his departure. Listen to Jesus' words to his disciples the night before he died, at the dinner with the foot-washing:

> But now I am going to him who sent me....I tell you the truth: it is to your advantage that I go away, for if I do not go away, the Helper will not come to you. But if I go, I will send him to you.[135]

Who is Jesus referring to as "the Helper"? He's speaking of the Holy Spirit, another member of the Trinity, along with Jesus and the Father. As we saw in part four, the God of the Bible is three, but also one. This means that when Jesus sent "the Helper," he sent *his* Spirit to be with us.

Jesus goes so far as to say that this is to our advantage. Jesus was present physically in one place, at one time. Though his Spirit he is with all of us, all of the time. The Spirit's role is to bring peace, comfort, and to continue to show us how to live like Jesus did. The Bible says that God is still *with* us. He never left, and he never will.

The Bible also teaches that Jesus' Spirit is not only *with* us, but *in* us. This means God's love and purpose is in those who trust and follow Jesus. The Christmas message didn't stop with Jesus, it continues in his followers. The Bible's New Testament teaches that the grace, mercy and kindness Jesus showed the world should extend through all who hold his name dear.

If phase one of God's plan was to send Jesus into the world to model humility, grace and love, then phase two is that Jesus' followers continue in this way of life. This means that little-old-ordinary you and I can join with God in bringing hope and healing to the world.

Christmas began with Jesus, but it continues through us.

Curtain call.

Back in part five we talked about that scene in *Home Alone* when Kevin is sent to his room without any dinner. At the end of *Home Alone*, Kevin's mother finally makes it back to her son after a long journey. Mother and son embrace and forgive one another, the whole family bursts through the door, and Kevin's overjoyed to see them.[136] I love that scene. It's a familiar kind of scene in films in general, but especially popular in Christmas movies:

Everyone comes back together.

Everyone who's previously been part of the story is reunited.

All gather under one roof, or around a Christmas tree, or a table.

Everyone's back home....and home is a good place.

When I watch our kids tell the Christmas story in plays at my church, my imagination kicks into overdrive. When I set up the family nativity scene on the mantelpiece every year, I can't help but wonder... What was it like to be at the manger, actually in the stable the night Jesus was born? What was it like to be a shepherd, to have actually seen Jesus in the flesh? What about a wise man, and to have laid gifts at his feet?

WHEN GOD WAS LITTLE

It must have been amazing to have been part of the cast of Christmas.

But what if (and I make no apology for this potentially cheesy metaphor), the casting call is still open, and the curtain call has been delayed?

What if we belong in, and can be part of the story, too?

Shepherds, wise men, teenage girls, carpenters, teachers, bankers, car salespeople, stay-at-home moms, stay-at-home dads, lawyers, mechanics, business people, road workers, hairstylists, grandparents, uncles, aunts, students, kids, poor people, rich people, nice people and Scrooges. What if we all have a place in the story?

The good news says that everyone can come home. Everyone belongs at the table. Everyone can join the cast. God was little in the person of Jesus, but his love is bigger than we can possibly imagine. There's plenty of room around the manger, and lots of space under the cross.

> Fear not, for behold, I bring you good news of great joy that will be for all the people. For unto you is born this day in the city of David a Saviour, who is Christ the Lord. And this will be a sign for you: you will find a baby wrapped in swaddling cloths and lying in a manger.[137]

When God was little he made room for us all. The question is, will we make room for him?

> Joy to the world, the Lord is come.
> Let earth receive her King.
> Let every heart prepare him room,
> And heaven and nature sing,
> And heaven and nature sing,
> And heaven and heaven and nature sing.[138]

www.whengodwaslittle.com

NOTES

PART ONE

1   McCutchan, R. G. (1937). *Our Hymnody*: A Manual of the
    Methodist Hymnal. New York, Cincinnati: The Methodist Book
    Concern.

2   To learn more about Jesus' historicity, see John Dickson's
    Investigating Jesus: A Historian's Quest (Oxford, Lion Hudson,
    2010).

3   His Holiness the Dalai Lama, *A Buddhist Perspective on the
    Teachings of Jesus*. (Massachusetts Wisdom Publications, 1996).

4   A recent documentary was produced about Vancouver,
    British Columbia and it's feelings about the Christian religion in
    particular (http://vimeo.com/31117591).

5   Everitt, Anthony. Augustus: *The Life of Rome's First Emperor*.
    (New York: Random House, 2006), 85.

6   For a comprehensive read on Jesus' staggering impact on the
    western world, read Ortberg, John, *Who is this Man? The Un
    predictable Impact of the Inescapable Jesus*, (Grand Rapids,
    Michigan: Zondervan, 2012).

7   Mark 6 is one of a number of examples where Jesus refuses
    to force belief on those he preaches to. Mark says that Jesus
    visited his hometown of Nazareth and was subsequently
    rejected there. Jesus didn't force the issue and moved on. This
    is characteristic of Jesus in the gospels. He doesn't force belief,
    but invites it.

8   Acts 14

9   Keller, Timothy, *The Reason for God: Belief in the Age of
    Skepticism*, (New York, New York: Penguin Group, 2008), 205.

10 Acts 17.22-25, paraphrase my own.

11   For further reading see John Walton's *Ancient Near Eastern Thought and the Old Testament: Introducing the Conceptual World of the Hebrew Bible* (Michigan, Baker Academic, 2006).

12   Mark 6. 30-44, Mark 8.1-10

13   For further reading see Provan, Long, Longman, *A Biblical History of Israel* (Kentucky, Westminster John Knox Press, 2003).

14   Mark 9. 36-37, paraphrase my own.

15   Exodus 20.13

16   Matthew 5.22

17   Ortberg, John, *Who is this Man? The Unpredictable Impact of the Inescapable Jesus*, (Grand Rapids, Michigan: Zondervan, 2012), 43.

18   Exodus 33.17-23

19   Exodus 20.4

20   Keller, Timothy, *Reasons for God: Belief in the Age of Skepticism*, (New York, New York: Penguin Group, 2008), 207.

21   Part four will look at some of these statements in greater detail.

22   C.S. Lewis's trilemma. Consider Lewis' *Mere Christianity* for an thoughtful defence of the Christian faith.

PART TWO

23   *Talladega Nights: The Ballad of Ricky Bobby.* Dir. Adam McKay. Pref. Will Ferrell. Columbia Pictures, 2006.

24   Jesus of Nazareth. Dir. Franco Zeffirelli. Pref. Robert Powell. ITC, RAI, 1977.

25   Matthew 1.1-17

26   Wessel, Walter Expositor's Bible Commentary: Mark. (Regency Reference Library, Michigan, 1984), 13.

27   Mark 1.1-3

28   Luke 1.3-4

29   *Star Wars Episode IV: A New Hope.* Dir. George Lucas. Twentieth Century Fox, 1977.

30   N.T. Wright. From a lecture in Langley, BC, November, 2010.

31   Dickens, Charles. *A Christmas Carol,* (London: Chapman and Hall, 1843).

32   John 1.1-5

33   Draper, Robert. *"Rethinking Nero" National Geographic* 2014 September: 82-111

34   Draper, Robert. *"Rethinking Nero" National Geographic* 2014 September: 82-111

35   Draper, Robert. *"Rethinking Nero" National Geographic* 2014 September: 82-111

36   Draper, Robert. *"Rethinking Nero" National Geographic* 2014 September: 82-111

37   Luke 20.46

38   Matthew 16.15

39   Matthew 1.1-17

40   Matthew 2

41   Matthew 21

42   Dickson, John. Humilitas: *A Lost Key to Life, Love, and Leadership.* (Grand Rapids, Michigan: Zondervan, 2011), chapter five.

43   Dickson, John. Humilitas: A *Lost Key to Life, Love, and Leadership.* (Grand Rapids, Michigan: Zondervan, 2011), chapter six.

44   *Spirituals Triumphant, Old and New.* 1927.

45   1 Peter 4.12-13

46   Philippians 2

47   Liefeld, Walter L. The Expositor's Bible Commentary: Luke
       (Regency Reference Library, Michigan, 1984), 844.

48   Luke 2.7

PART THREE

49   John 1.1

50   Barclay, William. *The Daily Bible Study Series: The Gospel of John
       Volume 1 Revised Edition.* (Westminster Press,
       Philadelphia, 1975), 26-50.

51   John's use of "logos" held significant meaning for both his Jewish
       and Greek audience. For the Greeks, "logos" meant (in part)
       the reason or mind of God, so John is stating that Jesus was the
       mind or reason of God explained. For more on this, see just
       about any Bible commentary on the Gospel of John.

52   Matthew 1.21

53   Isaiah 7.14

54   Hugh Halter at a retreat for pastors in Abbotsford, BC, Spring
       2014.

55   Mark 6.1-6

56   Psalm 34.18

57   Luke 14.12-14

58   Luke 2.8-16

59   Morris, Leon. *Tyndale New Testament Commentaries: The Gospel
       According to St. Luke* p.84 (William B. Eerdmans Publishing
       Company, Grand Rapids, Michigan, 1979).

60   Wright, N.T. *Following Jesus: Biblical Reflections on Discipleship* p. 66 (William B. Eerdmans Publishing Company, Grand Rapids, Michigan, 1995).

61   Luke 2.18

PART FOUR

62   Psalm 8.3-4

63   Genesis 1.1

64   Hebrews 1.1-3a

65   Colossians 1.15-17

66   Philippians 3.5-6

67   This is an obviously minimal treatment of a massive theological topic. For further reading on the Trinity, consider Darrell W. Johnson's *Experiencing the Trinity* (Regent College Publishing, Vancouver, 2002).

68   John 1.1-5

69   Genesis 1.1-3

70   John 8.12

71   John 1.14

72   John 19

73   John 20

74   Watts, Rikk. This thinking emerged from a sermon given at Living Waters Church in the fall of 2013.

75   1 John 2.23-24

76   Revelation 1.17-18

PART FIVE

77   Zach Galifianakis on *George Tonight* (CBC, 2010).

78   *The Dark Knight*. Dir. Christopher Nolan. Pref. Heath Ledger.
        Warner Bros, Legendary Pictures, Syncopy, DC Comics, 2008.

79   Kaiser, Jr. Walter C. *The Expositor's Bible Commentary: Exodus*
        (Regency Reference Library, Grand Rapids, Michigan, 1990), 309.

80   Exodus 1-3

81   Without diving into a complex discussion of the problem of pain
        and evil and the challenges they bring to belief in the God of the
        Bible (and thus getting away from our thesis) let me recommend
        John G. Stackhouse, Jr.'s thorough and compelling *Can God Be
        Trusted: Faith and the Challenge of Evil* (IVP Books, Downers
        Grove, Illinois, 2009).

82   For a helpful tool when studying the Bible I recommend Gordon
        Fee and Douglas Stuart's, *How to Read the Bible for all its Worth*.
        (Grand Rapids, Mihigan: Zondervan, 2003)

83   Mark 10.13-16

84   For an inspiring look at Jesus' influence on how we treat children
        today, read John Ortberg's, *Who is this Man? The Unpredictable
        Impact of the Inescapable Jesus,* (Grand Rapids, Michigan:
        Zondervan, 2012), chapter 3: *A Revolution in Humanity.*

85   Luke 15.1-10

86   Luke 15.11-32

87   Graves, Dan. *Did Robertson Wander as He Feared?* Christianity
        Today.com http://www.christianity.com/church/church-
        history/timeline/1701-1800/did-robert-robinson-wander-as-
        he-feared-11630313.html

88   Robinson, Robert, *Come, Thou Fount of Every Blessing*. 1957.

89   For tried and trusted reading on the broader Christian story, and
        it's logical appeal, read C.S. Lewis' *Mere Christianity* (1952).

90   For an in-depth consideration of this kind of biblical interpreta
      tion, read Webb, William J. *Slaves, Women, and Homosexuals:*
      Exploring the Hermeneutics of Cultural Analysis, (Downers Grove,
      Illinois: Intervarsity Press, 2001).

91   Galatians 4.4-7

92   The biblical book of Romans outlines this journey from Paul's
      perspective.

93   Romans 7.15

94   Matthew 23, Matthew 21.12-17, Mark 14.32-65

95   The story of the woman caught in adultery in John 8 is a good
      example of this.

96   Noah. Dir. Darren Aronofsky. Paramount Picture, Regency Enter
      prises, Protozola Pictures, Disruption Entertainment, 2014.

97   Romans 5

98   *Home Alone*. Dir. Chris Columbus. Hughes Entertainment,
      Twentieth Century Fox, 1990.

99   *Lawrence of Arabia*. Dir. David Lean. Pref. Claude Rains. Columbia
      Pictures, 1962.

100   Exodus 4.10

101   Exodus 3-15

102   Genesis 26.3

103   1 Samuel 17

104   1 Samuel 17.37

105   Psalm 23

PART SIX

106   Peterson, Eugene, *The Message*: John 1. 14, (Colorado Springs: Navpress, 2003).

107   Hebrews 1.3a

108   Colossians 1.15

109   Colossians 2.9

110   John 13-17

111   John 14.8-11

112   John 13.3-5

113   Watts, Rikk In a sermon on John's foot washing at Living Waters Church, Fort Langley in the spring of 2014.

114   John 13.6-9

115   John 13.12-16

116   Matthew 20.24-28

117   Dickson, John. *Humilitas: A Lost Key to Life, Love, and Leadership.* (Grand Rapids, Michigan: Zondervan, 2011), chapter six.

118   Philippians 2.3-11

119   Philippians 2.2 (NASV)

120   Charles Dickens, *A Christmas Carol*, 1843.

PART SEVEN

121   Dickson, John. Humilitas: *A Lost Key to Life, Love, and Leadership.* (Grand Rapids, Michigan: Zondervan, 2011).

122   Luke 19.1-10

123   Mark 2.17

124   Matthew 16.13-23

125   Luke 22.24-34

126   John 13.5-9

127   Matthew 26. 36-46, Mark 14. 32-42, Luke 22. 39-46

128   John 18.1-11

129   Matthew 26.47-56

130   Matthew 26, Mark 14, Luke 22, John 18.

131   John 6.41-66

132   John 6.68

133   Matthew 28, Mark 16, Luke 24, John 20

134   Acts 1 Jesus' ascension to the heavens again points to the first Christians' view that he was divine.

135   John 16.5-7

136   *Home Alone*. Dir. Chris Columbus. Hughes Entertainment, Twentieth Century Fox, 1990.

137   Luke 2.10-12

138   Isaac Watts, "*Joy to the World*". *The Psalms of David: Imitated in the language of the New Testament*. 1719.